# THE ROOTS OF TICASUK

TICASUK (Emily Ivanoff Brown) was born in Unalakleet, Alaska, in 1904. Her mother was Iñupiaq and her father was of Russian-American-English heritage. After earning her teacher's certificate in Oregon, she taught in Kotzebue for two years and then attended nursing school in Seattle so she could address health issues in Alaska Native villages. She married Robert Brown, whom she met in Seattle, and they had three sons. She taught in Kotzebue and Unalakleet schools for over thirty years and was an early promoter of bilingual education. She received many awards for her work in education and preserving Native culture: the Governor's Award, Alaskan of the Year, 1969; Distinguished Alumnus of the Year, University of Alaska, 1970; Woman of the Year, National Federation of Press Women, 1974; and a Presidential Commendation for "exceptional service to others in the finest American tradition," from President Nixon. She received her honorary Doctor of Humanities degree posthumously, six days after her death.

ELAINE CHUKAN BROWN serves as a public speaker, wine writer, and consultant on mentorship, diversity, and equity programs worldwide. As a grandchild of Ticasuk, Brown works to raise awareness and understanding of Indigenous peoples and issues unique to their communities. Brown has served as a cultural advisor for book projects, university courses, organizations, events, and television shows. As a wine writer, Brown has served as the Executive Editor US for *JancisRobinson.com*, a columnist for *Decanter*, a contributing writer to multiple books and magazines, and co-founded the Diversity in Wine Leadership Forum. A board member for the Wine Writers' Symposium, Brown splits time between Alaska and Sonoma, California, where they live with their pet guinea pigs, rabbit, hamster, and Rosie bird.

# THE ROOTS OF TICASUK

**TICASUK
(EMILY IVANOFF BROWN)**

*Emily Ivanoff Brown*

Foreword by
**ELAINE CHUKAN BROWN**

NORTHWEST
COLLECTION
*Portland, Oregon*

ABOUT THE RESTORATION

Original files and/or page proofs for *The Roots of Ticasuk* were no longer available. An out-of-print edition of the book was photographed and scanned to create a new digital manuscript. Errors created in the scanning process, as well as typographical errors in the original edition, were corrected. Though slight changes were made to terminology and layout of the appendices, this new edition includes all of the material that appeared in the original publication and preserves the author's original language, orthography, and chapter and section titles.

Restoration supervisor: Dan DeWeese
Cultural and linguistic consultant: Elaine Chukan Brown
Digitization process: Rachel Greben

THIS IS A NORTHWEST COLLECTION TITLE
PUBLISHED BY PROPELLER BOOKS
4325 NORTHEAST DAVIS STREET, PORTLAND, OR 97213
www.propellerbooks.com

All author proceeds from sales of this book go to the Emily Brown Learning Center at the University of Alaska Fairbanks Northwest Campus in Nome, Alaska.

Cover photo of Ticasuk courtesy Elaine Chukan Brown
Cover and interior design by Dan DeWeese

ISBN 978-1-95559-311-3

10 9 8 7 6 5 4 3 2 1

THE NORTHWEST COLLECTION is a series of titles that represent the rich literary history of the Pacific Northwest, published in editions featuring introductions and insights from contemporary writers.

# CONTENTS

Foreword                                                    vii

Acknowledgments                                             xxi

Introduction                                              xxiii

PART I: ALLUYAGNAK AND FAMILY

1 Masu Smuggles the Indian Boy                               1

2 Masu Adopts the Indian Boy                                 5

3 Nulthkutuk's Training                                      9

4 Nulthkutuk Becomes Chief                                  15

PART II: MALQUAY

5 Malquay's Youth                                           25

6 Malquay's First Visit to St. Michael                      29

7 Malquay Encounters a Strange Culture                      39

8 Homeward Bound                                            43

PART III: CHALAVALUK

9 Chalavaluk                                                51

10 Infanticide                                              57

11 Chalavaluk's Adventure                                   61

12 Chalavaluk Begins a New Life                             67

PART IV: CHIKUK

13 Chikuk's Wish                                            73

14 Chikuk's Engagement and Wedding                          75

15 Yukuniagag & Ahlugga Hunt Sea Mammals                    81

16 Sergei's Curiosity                                       85

17 Sunset for Chikuk                                        89

## PART V: STEPHAN AND MALQUAY

18 Arrival of the Reverend Karlson      105
19 Stephan and Malquay      111

## APPENDICES

Appendix I: Six Generations of Ticasuk's
     Extended Family      115
Appendix II: Ticasuk's Family Tree      116
Iñupiaq-English Glossary      118

# FOREWORD

My grandmother gave me two dolls. The first was handstitched from seal skin and fur, dressed in traditional parka and mukluks and made by one of the Iñupiaq elders of our region in northern Alaska. "So you know our people," she said. Then she sat with me on her bedside and told me about the village where she was born.

The second she gave me shortly before she died. It was a doll handmade entirely of yarn by a Black woman she befriended on one of her trips through the United States. The body of the doll was brown yarn, and her dress and hat were pink crochet. "So you know other people," she said. Then she told me that eventually I would travel too, that she wanted me to be curious, and good at listening. I was eight years old.

These two views—to know your people, and to learn from others—exemplified my grandmother, Emily Ivanoff Brown, as well as the meaning of her Iñupiaq name, Ticasuk. Directly translated, a *ticasuk* is a hollow in the ground where the four winds gather. But the larger meaning alludes to wisdom and treasure from cultures around the world finding a home in the ticasuk. Through her work and travels, she fulfilled the meaning of her name.

Teaching Indigenous students of Alaska was her life work, and upholding Indigenous culture was her passion. Her heritage preservation efforts made her one of the first Alaska Native writers in the state. Only the book *The People of Kauwerak* by William Oguilluk of Point Hope was published before her, in 1973. Ticasuk had already self-published several chapbooks on the Indigenous history of Alaska, and the origins of the naniq, a traditional stone and oil lamp, and the building styles of Iñupiaq homes. Then, in 1974, her master's thesis, *Grandfather of Unalakleet*, an oral narrative on the founding of her village was published. In 1981, it was reprinted as the book you hold now, *The Roots of Ticasuk*.

Ticasuk was the first to capture traditions of Norton Sound in writing and to publish its most unique legend, *Qayaq: The Longest Story Ever Told.* The story of Qayaq is an oral narrative told for so many generations no one knows when it started. Elders shared it through the dark of winter, over not only days, but months. It is a magical origin story as much as a lesson in listening, respect for the natural environment, and healthy living.

In 1987, a collection of myths and legends Ticasuk's mom told her was published as *Tales of Ticasuk*.

Ticasuk taught others that helping non-Natives learn the value of Indigenous peoples could be a means to preserving culture by garnering broader support.

"Let's help them see who we are," she said. "Because of the fact that outsiders don't know how we lived in the past, they think we are just primitive people. Our way of life has never been written as it should be, and so this is my life work. This has been my purpose: to try to retrieve and preserve this beautiful literature we have that is basically unknown."

## Childhood

Ticasuk was born in February 1904, in the village of Unalakleet along the coast of Alaska's Norton Sound, where her parents originated. Her father, Stephan Ivanoff, was the son of one of the first marriages in the region between a Russian man and a Yupik woman. Ticasuk's mother, Malquay, was a Malemiut Iñupiaq woman raised in a local orphanage after her parents died. Stephan and Malquay's unique backgrounds combined to create a family simultaneously invested in education and honoring their Indigenous people.

Born between two cultures, Stephan combined the worldview of his father with the traditions of his mother to aid his region. He spoke both Yupik and Iñupiaq in multiple dialects and served as a translator for diplomats and political leaders traveling northwestern Alaska. He founded the village of Shaktoolik outside Unalakleet, as well as its first school. He served as boat builder, started a series of camp houses for travelers along Norton Sound, and was a commissioner for the U.S. Bureau of Indian Affairs (BIA) for the Alaska territory's northern region. And he herded reindeer.

In the late 1800s, a boat was marooned in ice on the northeastern border of the Alaskan territory, stranding dozens of travelers through winter. Stephan led his reindeer from Shaktoolik along the Yukon River and over the Brooks Range to provide food and clothing for the boat travelers, covering more than seven hundred sixty miles on foot to reach them. He then left his reindeer with them and walked seven hundred sixty miles back.

When a missionary from the Swedish Covenant church arrived at Norton Sound, Stephan helped him settle, and then became one of his first students. The mentorship led Stephan to travel to North Park College in Chicago. There he studied music and business, constructed his own violin, and toured the United States playing to raise money for his education and the church. While at North Park he created more than one hundred and twenty drawings of his home region, one of which still hangs in the college, the rest of which now reside in the archives of the Smithsonian.

The work of missionaries in Alaska was bittersweet for Ticasuk. Her father was taught by the first missionaries in Norton Sound. Later, he became one for the region himself. Ticasuk understood that their influence caused cultural damage, yet she worked to understand them.

"The missionaries have destroyed our beautiful traditional customs," she said. "In my case, I am sorry that they did. But I do not blame them because they didn't study first about the way we lived, and it took them years to know how they not-knowingly destroyed our traditions."

Malquay clung to her Iñupiaq customs. Without her parents, she was taught local traditions, daily practices, Indigenous foods, myths and legends by the regional elders. With Stephan, she migrated between seasonal homes: the inland hills for squirrels and rabbit in springtime; the ocean shore for coho in summer; the banks of the Yukon for minks, ducks, and sockeye in early fall; trapping and hunting later in autumn and into the end of the year for ptarmigan, fox, lynx, moose, and caribou; then back to the village for winter. Each seasonal home added to the annual supply.

Malquay sewed fur for winter parkas, boots, traditional headdresses, and jewelry. As outsiders traveled Norton Sound, extra furs were sold or traded. Ducks, moose, caribou, lynx, salmon, squirrels, and tundra plants became food for winter. Eggs from seagulls, terns, and ducks kept through the cold months in an underground cache.

Malquay taught Ticasuk the Iñupiaq language, the history of the region, the oral narratives of their people, what tundra plants were safe to eat, and how to cook and sew. Stephan also taught Ticasuk English. Her uncle, Mischa, provided her first formal education at the school founded by her father.

Then, at the age of nine, the BIA took Ticasuk to Chemawa, an Indian Boarding School more than 2000 miles away. She remained until age twenty, unable to return home due to distance, and completed both high school and a teaching certificate. When she returned to Unalakleet, Ticasuk had lost Iñupiaq. The United States made speaking Indigenous languages in BIA schools a punishable offense beginning in the 1880s. The law remained intact until the 1970s.

The conditions of the Indian Boarding School impacted

Ticasuk's ongoing health. Over her life, she suffered multiple bouts of life-threatening flu, was hospitalized for tonsilitis, survived multiple forms of cancer, and escaped death at least three times.

Ticasuk married soon after completing her studies at Chemawa, bringing her husband with her to Alaska. She gave birth to three boys and a girl, losing her daughter to illness in infancy.

In her thirties, an epidemic of tuberculous pushed through remote Alaska, killing people throughout the state. When Ticasuk contracted the disease she developed internal hemorrhaging and was sent to a sanitarium, expected to die. Believing he'd lost his wife, her husband adopted one son to regional shopkeepers, left the others with Ticasuk's parents, and moved from Alaska. When Ticasuk unexpectedly recovered, she returned to Unalakleet to find her husband, the shopkeepers, and her infant gone from the region. It took almost thirty years for Ticasuk to reunite with her adopted son.

In her forties, Ticasuk developed pneumonia and went into a coma. Unable to transport her themselves, villagers raised an alert to passersby, a black blanket on a flagpole. Soon after, the pilot of a small plane spotted the blanket and flew Ticasuk to the hospital in Nome. There she was pronounced dead before managing to recover.

Later, while working in Kotzebue, Ticasuk suffered a stroke that left her in a coma. She was airlifted to a hospital in Fairbanks and during a surgery meant to repair damage from the stroke, she medically died on the table. Doctors manually massaged her heart, and again she miraculously recovered.

## Teaching Alaska

Ticasuk taught at BIA schools throughout northern Alaska for more than thirty years. In her first years home, she worked to relearn Iñupiaq. The experience gave her a realization. If it took only ten years for her to lose her language, an entire culture could be lost in one generation. Ticasuk realized the world was changing and her people needed additional skills to adapt.

"I saw the vastness of education and wanted to help my people. Without education, you cannot improve yourself physically, mentally and spiritually," she said. "Education is a preparation for life situations and changes. It takes determination to reach your goals faithfully and consistently. Education helps you learn that."

Ticasuk's teaching methods were unique. Like her mother, Ticasuk used the natural environment to show students what plants were safe to eat or had medicinal properties. She helped them learn how to work with the landscape for shelter or gathering food. And after foraging mushrooms, plants, and berries, she taught the students how to prepare them and bring them home to feed the village elders. At the same time, she founded Women's Clubs in villages where she taught or visited, creating a network throughout northern Alaska. The Women's Clubs guided members in foraging and cooking, tanning hides and sewing traditional garments, and served as a resource connecting women from different villages throughout the state.

Her teaching was not without controversy. The BIA provided teaching materials familiar to those in the continental United States. But Ticasuk found that the stories of dogs, cats, farms, and even tying shoelaces were nonsensical to village students. They had a lifestyle based in gathering food and resources from the rivers, ocean, and the land. Animals were for hunting or transport and almost never pets. And clothing was made of animal skins and fur, without shoelaces.

So, to help her students, Ticasuk began to write the myths, legends, and stories her mother told her. These became the teaching materials of her classroom, alongside daily outdoor excursions. In this way, Ticasuk developed some of the first bilingual curriculum in the territory, reasoning that students could only learn English if it was translated through their own language. She also told students stories in their own language and helped translate them to English.

Ticasuk's mother taught her that traditional stories were both educational and entertaining, and Ticasuk used this in her teaching. "That's the way we teach children," she said. "We have legends that represent how you can be good, and we have legends on the other side. The legends teach how to respect animals, the water, the land, and your family. If you are forgetful of the teachings, you suffer the consequences of being so forgetful and careless. This is the children's education." The approach effectively preserved the students' own language and culture in the classroom while also teaching them English and traditions from the rest of the United States.

National holidays were part of BIA education. Teaching students about Halloween one autumn, Ticasuk told them stories about spirits we must respect that live in the natural landscape. That night, one of her students had trouble sleeping and told his mother it was from his teacher's scary stories. The mother complained to the BIA school director, not about Iñupiaq curriculum, but about her child's fear. But the complaint revealed Ticasuk's bilingual education, a violation of national policy and she was fired the day after Halloween.

Ticasuk was well-known throughout northern Alaska for her work with students, village elders, and the members of Women's Clubs. When residents of the region heard of her firing, they marched to the school in protest, continuing the effort until she was reinstated. Ticasuk was the first educator under the BIA to honor Iñupiaq ways while also teaching students lessons needed for the broader world. Her work demonstrated the effectiveness of bilingual education, and the protests instigated dialogues that questioned the ban against Native languages. These discussions worked towards eventually changing the regulation.

Speaking Indigenous languages in schools remained illegal for decades. The policy worked as originally intended. Most of the subsequent generations failed to speak their languages into adulthood. Many (including my parents) could understand their language when spoken to by their elders but could only respond in English. Their children retained neither.

## Ticasuk's Adult Education

At the age of fifty, Ticasuk sought to broaden her abilities for cultural preservation work and began taking summer school classes at the University of Alaska in pursuit of a bachelor's degree. In the meantime, she taught in Unalakleet, Shaktoolik, White Mountain, Arctic Slope, Meade River, Noatak, Shageluk, Kotzebue, and elsewhere. While in Kotzebue she worked to establish the region's first public library. The village was without funds for the effort, so Ticasuk wrote a chapbook on the Indigenous history of Alaska, invested her own money to have it printed, then sold copies as a fundraiser. Her book raised enough to start the library and bring in books for the villagers to read.

Her undergraduate education, she reasoned, would help her gain legitimacy with outsiders while also developing the skills she needed to write more. "I managed to pass," she said. "I wanted to show them I was made of good stuff." After ten years of summer school, she completed her bachelor's in education.

Ticasuk retired from teaching and turned to pursuing higher education full-time, beginning a master's in communication, while also completing a second bachelor's in Iñupiaq. Then she began doctoral work. She paid for her studies working as a counselor at the university, helping Native students from throughout the state adjust to campus.

In her determination to raise support for cultural preservation, Ticasuk founded the Alaska Heritage Writer's Association and served as its director. The association gathered people from throughout Alaska working to preserve its history, including writers of all ethnicities and backgrounds. She also spoke to politicians, diplomats, leaders, directors, and educators throughout Alaska and the United States to increase awareness of issues unique to Indigenous peoples and to encourage funding for preservation work.

While at the university, she partnered with professors to create the first Iñupiaq bilingual curriculum for other educators in Alaska, co-wrote the first Iñupiaq-English dictionary in her mother's Malemiut Iñupiaq dialect, transcribed an Iñupiaq song collection, and dictated most of an encyclopedia on Yupik and Iñupiaq uses for regional plants. Her efforts helped instigate the university's creation of the state's first Alaska Native Studies degree program.

Ticasuk published multiple books in her lifetime, one posthumously, and donated numerous papers, audio recordings, and extensive research to the university archives with the hope others would continue her cultural work.

## National Recognition

Ticasuk's work led to honors from throughout the country. During her teaching career, she was repeatedly named best primary teacher, or best educator in the northern region. As she moved into her publishing work, she received numerous scholarships and fellowships to fund her research.

In 1970, she was named the Distinguished Alumnus of the year for University of Alaska. The same year, a Pulitzer Prize-winning journalist donated funds to the university to start the Emily Ivanoff Brown scholarship for Indigenous students, awarded each semester. A few months later, she received news from the White House. The President of the United States was awarding her "a citation for outstanding service to others for many years of work in teaching, writing, and public service to her fellow Alaskans." She was flown to Washington, D.C. and given the award by President Nixon.

In 1972, the Women's National Farm & Garden Association granted her funding to encourage her research and writing in cultural preservation. In 1974, she co-won the Woman of the Year award from the National Federation of Press Women. It was given to Ticasuk "for her contributions to cultural pride, the education of young Alaskan Natives, and preservation of traditional stories." She received telegrams from the governor of Alaska and its senators congratulating her for the award. The Alaska Press Women's Association raised money to fly Ticasuk to attend the award ceremony in Bismarck, North Dakota. The recognition was given to her alongside Katherine Graham, publisher of the Washington Post, for breaking the story on the Watergate Scandal.

The Alaska Legislature awarded Ticasuk citations two different times for "the preservation of Alaska Native culture." The Alaska Press Club named her for their annual civic award multiple years. When *Roots of Ticasuk* was published in 1981, the *Seattle Times* wrote in their review, "Once in a while, a little book comes along that deserves an honored place on the Alaskana shelf. […] *Roots of Ticasuk* is one." Another review named her "the Alex Haley of Alaska," stating that her work was as important to Alaska Native culture as his was for African American history.

In spring of 1982, the Alaska Library Association gave Ticasuk a commendation "for her special contribution to Alaska letters." Soon after, Governor Jay Hammond awarded her a special citation for her dedication to Alaska and its heritage. Then the university informed her they were awarding her an honorary doctorate of humanities for her lifetime of study and cultural preservation work. She died of cancer in May 1982, a few days before the ceremony.

Ticasuk was survived by three children, nine grandchildren and a great-grandchild as well as by an immeasurable number of students, mentees, and people she inspired. The day after her burial, a second great-grandchild was born. More have followed since, furthering her legacy.

## Ticasuk's Legacy

Recognition of Ticasuk's work continued even after her passing. Her obituary was written by former professor and mentor Jimmy Bedford. In it he remarked, "Her legacy to Alaska

Natives is enormous but all Alaskans are in her debt." He went on to list her national accomplishments, as well.

Funeral services were held throughout Alaska. The University of Alaska welcomed hundreds of people to a celebration of her life. It included recognition of a commemorative naniq she designed for campus as a celebration of Alaska Native cultures and a welcome to new Native students. About the naniq, Ticasuk had once explained, "For Indigenous people, the naniq is a symbol of light in the darkness as well as a stove to cook food. It is a reminder to Natives of their heritage." Today, the university naniq is dedicated to her memory, is lit through the winter months, and to open the first day of a new semester.

In Anchorage, her celebration of life lasted several hours. The church was filled with mourners who took over the middle of the service telling stories of how Ticasuk changed their life. One attendee explained that he'd only met Ticasuk once, more than ten years before. That day, he said, he was drunk at a bus stop. Ticasuk sat beside him and they talked long enough for her to miss her bus. The next day, he said, he stopped drinking, and credited their conversation for him deciding to be sober.

Ticasuk was buried where she was born, in Unalakleet. Within a few years, the village opened a public library in her honor.

The Northwest Community College of Nome dedicated the Emily Ivanoff Brown Student Resource Center in 1983. Later, the college became the northwest campus of the University of Alaska, and a second dedication ceremony was held including her extended family and numerous people she mentored from throughout the state.

Outside Fairbanks, the Emily Ticasuk Brown Elementary school was dedicated in 1987. Her sons and grandchildren (including me) attended, as well as members of the state legislature whom she had previously taught, and multiple former students. When the school opened, it included one of the state's preeminent special education programs, and the first in the region to bring special education within the purview of a mainstream school.

In 2009, Ticasuk was added to the Alaska Women's Hall of Fame.

Besides Ticasuk's writing, she was one of the first to mentor others to also write their own traditions. In this way, she expanded the effort to preserve Alaska Native heritage far beyond her own work. Her example inspired numerous other Indigenous writers both inside and beyond the state. Her love and guidance also helped me fulfill the meaning of my Indigenous name, *Arnaqiaq*, the little woman born already grown up, that she may share the insights of her people.

\*\*\*

During Ticasuk's lifetime, use of the word *Eskimo* was standard practice in reference to numerous coastal groups in both Alaska and northern Canada. The word from its origins is a slur. Even so, its use was mandated by the United States government, as well as previously by the Canadian government, and today remains the legal name used federally in the U.S. as well as linguistically in relation to several language families. It is strongly recommended that anyone not a member of Indigenous groups to whom the word was applied avoid using it.

Until a little before the last decade, tribal names such as *Yupik* or *Iñupiaq* were not generally known outside their Indigenous communities. Because non-Natives tended to be unaware of specific tribal names, it was customary for them to refer to western and northern coastal tribal groups of Alaska as *Eskimo*. Re-educating people to using appropriate tribal names continues to be an ongoing process and had made little progress during my grandmother's lifetime.

*The Roots of Ticasuk* was unprecedented when it was published. It is also a restoration of oral traditions from Norton Sound that would have been lost without my grandmother's effort. In another way, it is a window to another time not only through the story she tells, but also for how her use of a slur to describe her people exemplifies the limitations in outside understanding at the time. She made a compromise to be understood by a larger audience with the hope to deepen their support of heritage preservation. The uncomfortable reference demonstrates her commitment to ensure her people will know their history while she seeks to expand the community of those who support such work. She chose to write in ways they could understand. The hope was that in taking this first step, respect for her culture would continue to improve over time.

For her work and expansive view, I am grateful to my grandmother. In respect for her and how much she accomplished, the publisher and I have chosen to leave *The Roots of Ticasuk* as she wrote it.

Proceeds from the sale of this book will be given to the Emily Ivanoff Brown Student Resource Center at the northwest campus of the University of Alaska in Nome. We reprint this book in recognition of her dedication to mentoring new students and most of all to honor her ancestors as well as her extended family and offspring.

ELAINE CHUKAN BROWN
*For Melvin, Sydney, and Leonard*

# ACKNOWLEDGMENTS

*Quyahnaa*—thanks—to Carrie Soxie and her son, Franklin, who passed on to me the oral history of our family. I have the greatest admiration for Carrie for her knowledge of Nulthkutuk, a hero who saved our line from extermination and insured the survival of the Iñupiaq Eskimos at Unalakleet to this century.

My thanks also go to those educators and citizens who have contributed so much in bringing a new way of life to the Natives of Alaska and who taught us to be a part of the great democracy of the United States of America.

Thanks to the many professors at the University of Alaska, especially Charles J. Keim and Jimmy Bedford, who helped me learn about America and its culture.

There were many financial contributions made to me by the Women's National Farm and Garden Association, Inc., of Detroit, Michigan, and I am deeply grateful to Mary Jane Fate and Ida Greiner for assistance in arranging this support for my masters degree program, which led to the completion of this book. And special thanks to Janet Brunberg and Virginia Heiner, who were especially helpful in the final editing.

Lastly, but not least, thanks to my God who gave me much encouragement.

*Quyahnaa* to you all.

TICASUK
(Emily Ivanoff Brown)

# INTRODUCTION

ONE DAY years ago Nee Appangak (Mrs. Carrie Soxie), the daughter of Delialuk by his second wife, Kotogan, told me of the great chief Alluyagnak I and his descendants.

"Our ancestors," she began, "migrated here from the Kobuk Valley. They were the Kuvunmute—Kobuk People—and they were Indian-Eskimo. The Kuvunmute moved southward, passing by Seelvik Kangik and Immitchak. Some settled in Koyuk along the Norton Bay. Indeed, my parents celebrated festivals with your grandfather Qunigrak's parents in Koyuk. But more of the Kuvunmute moved on than stayed, for their leader thought it unwise to live so far from the main ocean and sea mammals.

"They moved north to Pastolik, but as they could not speak the language of the natives there, they moved again and settled on the west sandbank of the Unalakleet River. Their descendants are the Unalakleets.

"One of your great, great, great-grandfathers was the chief Alluyagnak I, whose maiden sister adopted an orphaned Indian boy. The child was then named Alluyagnak II, and he became a great chief for his new people. He saved them from destruction by enemy Indians and, thus, preserved our lineage. You and I may not have been born had it not been for the wisdom of Alluyagnak II. He had five sons,* and their names were Delialuk, Maktak, Taktuk, Paniptchuk, and Nashoalook…

* In truth, four or more generations were between Alluyagnak II and these five "sons."

Hearing of my ancestors in Nee Appangak's stories has been a deeply rewarding experience for me. It has strengthened a kinship between my relatives and me and given me a pride in my heritage. It is sad to think that many of my people have missed this experience, for unfortunately, the people of the Unalakleet region have not been able to preserve their history. Much of it is already lost. The natives had no written language, and since the coming of the white man, the tales have not been carefully passed from one generation to the next.

I wish that my descendants may know who their people are. To this end I attended the University of Alaska to learn enough of the humanities, social sciences, folklore, and mythology that I might properly preserve in writing the culture of my people.

I have set out to show the people of Unalakleet are one through the lineage of Alluyagnak I.

# I

# ALLUYAGNAK AND FAMILY

# 1
# MASU SMUGGLES THE INDIAN BOY

AFTER THEIR successful battle with the Indians of Interior Alaska, the Unalakleet warriors were not aware of any Indian survivors. No one in this Eskimo community on the Bering Sea Coast suspected that one person had survived, and there was a great celebration.

The day following the celebration, the chief's sister, Masu, was the only one who gave thought to the aftermath of the battle. She left the village early in the morning to salvage the remains of the snares at the battlefield. No one knew when she left. On her way she picked berries until she filled her pack and she left it near the path to retrieve on her way back. Then she continued on to the scene of the battle. When she arrived at the bank of the river, she decided to rest and eat her lunch. While she sat eating, she heard a cough from the other side of the river. She listened...then she heard it again. She was quite sure that it was a human cough, and she immediately waded across the water. Climbing the river bank, she heard the cough again. This time it sounded closer. She walked in the direction of the sound, and each time the cough was repeated she was guided closer to the source. In this way she walked among the trees until she found an Indian boy lying under a spruce tree on a bed of spruce boughs. He appeared to be about seven years old. Lacking a sleeping bag to keep warm, he was shivering and coughing uncontrollably. Masu went over and sat beside him. She could not speak to him for she was overwhelmed with pity for the starving, helpless boy. He watched anxiously for her next move. She managed to smile comfortingly at him, hoping that he would understand that she would not harm him. He cried silently.

Masu patted his shoulder, and he stopped crying when she showed her friendliness. In sign language, she offered her help. Then she ran down to the river to get some water. After he drank the water, she built a fire to warm him and gave him some of her food. Masu dried his wet clothes by rubbing and fanning them around the fire. When he had revived, she took him down to the river's edge and already she was beginning to lay plans for his future. She asked him if he would like to live with her at her village. It was difficult for her to convey her message to him, and he was fearful of mistreatment that might be inflicted upon him by other Eskimos. She explained to him that she would hide him in her igloo. She told him that they would travel after dark, and that no one would see them when they arrived at the village. He hesitated briefly, crying, and finally nodded his head. Neither could guess what future lay ahead for him when he accepted this adoption by one of the enemies of his people.

While they were traveling slowly toward the village, Masu decided to hide him in her winter clothes closet. In the morning, she would bring fresh berries to her brother, the chief, for she knew salmonberries were his favorite fruit. Then she would present her request to him. "Oh!" she whispered to her blackfish amulet, "Pray, help me to be granted my wish by my brother. Please soften his heart and make him understand that I love this helpless Indian boy." As they neared the village she said to the boy, "Let's rest for a while before we attempt to sneak to my igloo."

As they rested in the dark, he watched her empty the berries on her gut rain parka. Then she wiped her pack with moss until it was clean. She went to the boy and made a motion for him to get inside the pack. He obediently climbed into it, and after he had cuddled comfortably, she covered him with her outer parka. In that way, she was able to smuggle her future son into the village. And the Indian boy felt secure while she carried him on her back to his future home.

## 2
# MASU ADOPTS THE INDIAN BOY

MASU PLANNED her morning schedule before she fell aslep. After breakfast she would mix Eskimo ice cream and prepare some food for the Indian boy. Before she left she would warn him in sign language not to leave his hiding place while she was at her brother's home.

She resolved to get up earlier than usual to do her work while the boy was asleep. She would make careful preparations for her approach to her brother with her request for permission to adopt the boy. She resolved to be calm and especially tactful in her attitude and actions as she presented her request. Masu finally fell asleep.

When she got up she quietly started the work she had planned. The only interruption was an unexpected visit from her niece, Aligak, the chief's daughter. Fortunately, the girl sat still while Masu mixed the ice cream. The boy remained hidden, but peeped through the skin curtain to watch. Masu felt relieved when she finished mixing the whipped Eskimo ice cream, using the salmon-berries she had gathered. For then she could say, "Aligak, I'll have lunch with you and your father this noon. Would you like to take this to your house?" She filled an extra dish with luscious dessert.

"Yes, Auntie," Aligak answered with pleasure.

When Aligak left, Masu permitted the Indian boy to come

out of hiding and eat the remainder of the ice cream. As Masu handed him the dish, she smiled. She felt assured that he would not run away.

Masu was uneasy when she entered her brother's house. The table was already set and in the midst of it, their favorite dessert was laid. Her brother thanked her for the treat as they sat down to eat. Masu had no appetite, for she was worried. She tried not to reveal her anxiety, but her brother sensed it. The old chief said to her, "Masu, are you worried or unhappy about something?"

"I'm quite all right, brother. But may I speak with you after lunch? I have a favor to ask of you."

The old chief answered her immediately, "Your request is granted, my sister."

After lunch, the chief asked his daughter to go out and play. He left the table, and Masu followed him to his favorite chair. She listened as he asked her politely, "May I present my request first?" It is an Eskimo custom that men always speak first.

"*Ah* [yes]."

"I am an old man now, and will soon leave you and my daughter, Aligak. Take good care of my daughter and property. When Aligak is of age, you can present to her my will. After she's married she can live in my igloo. In the meantime, store all my hunting equipment, kitchen utensils, and furs away, so none of them will be ruined by exposure. Aligak will use her mother's things for patterns when she learns to sew and her future husband will have my hunting equipment.

"Be sure to encourage and give guidance to our people when they hunt and perform their other duties." He paused then. "If there are other important matters that I have not mentioned, feel free to consult me. Now, what is your request?"

Masu did not expect such an exchange of requests. Gripped with emotion, she made a special effort to regain her normal self-control once more. She accepted his "will" and promised to fulfill his wishes. Then it was time to make her request. She had confidence in her brother's ingenuity, for he was wise and honest in dealing with people's problems.

She related to him all that had happened on her trip to the battlefield. However, toward the climax of her story, when she was about to tell of the predicament of the Indian boy she had rescued, she could not suppress her anxiety. She thought of the amulet, so she urged it to give her courage, poise, and strength at this critical time.

"Oh, chief! You know that I have lived a lonely life without a family; no son nor daughter to rear. When I die our lineage will end. And who will continue to serve our people? Please, let me adopt the boy. If you don't grant my request, the village warriors will kill him. I promise that tutors will be hired to teach him how to become a great hunter. Further, after I die, he will naturally become a chief. Our people need a man to rely on, rather than a helpless woman like me."

"*Tavra* [enough]!" he said. "Listen to me, Masu. You are a wise woman. I know your concern for our future. Your request is granted. Tonight I will give you the right to adopt the boy. Also, I will christen him with my name. We will celebrate the adoption with a special function in honor of our future chief, your son. But we will not reveal all our plans tonight, because opposition might arise from our people. The story will be related as it happened to you first, and I will introduce him to the people after I christen him," planned the old chief.

'Masu, you send for my messenger immediately. He can convey the message to our people of our plans for a celebration." The chief's face beamed as he envisioned his successor.

"May the ruler of our sky, Selam Inua, bring happiness and wisdom to you and your adopted son," the old chief gave his blessing to Masu with his arms uplifted. After he shook her hand, Masu expressed her appreciation.

"*Quyahnaa* [thank you]."

They parted, but only to make preparations for the ceremony to mark the introduction of the future chief. Masu went to her igloo immediately after she summoned the messenger. In sign language, she related her message to the happy Indian boy.

"Tomorrow, you'll become a member of our group. You will be permitted to meet your new friends. They will teach you many Eskimo games, and you will show them how to whittle toys," Masu told him.

He may have wanted to express his thankfulness in words at the moment; instead all he could do was hug his foster mother. Tears of happiness welled within the eyes of both. Masu withdrew first and said, "My brother, the chief of our village, will give you a new name. Hereafter, I shall call you by that name. Your name will be Nulthkutuk, a great Eskimo chief's name. Tonight, my people, your new relatives, will celebrate the day of a new addition to the community.

"We must prepare for the feasting and dancing. And beginning tomorrow, you shall be instructed in the Eskimo language. After you learn to talk fluently, you'll learn to be a great hunter and warrior."

Masu was sorry that she had mentioned the word *warrior*, because it reminded him of his unhappy experience. To rectify the situation, Masu changed the subject and said to him, "Let's get ready for the big feast. First, I will prepare new clothing for you, and while I'm busy with that, here is a new knife for you. You can whittle cottonwood bark and carve Indian toys."

The future chief's training was soon to begin, training which would in time help to guide a powerful, wise leader of the Eskimo people of Unalakleet.

# 3
# NULTHKUTUK'S TRAINING

THE DAY after the celebration, Masu and Unag, the tutor, drew up Nulthkutuk's educational program for the coming year. To solve the problem of communication, it was decided to teach him the Iñupiaq language first. Then he would continue his education in the fall by working as an apprentice for a skilled craftsman.

Most of his lessons would mainly involve listening to and observing the chosen craftsman. Masu and Unaq decided it would help him learn the language more quickly if they selected a companion who would involve him in the activities in the village. The boy would practice how to pronounce the names of things by imitating his companion, and he would acquire the art of listening. His companion could also teach him to make clay and sand models of community equipment, such as the umiak, the kayak and the dog sled. He would enjoy the companionship of other boys and girls and be encouraged to play games and compete in the village sports.

When winter came and the rivers, lakes, and sea were frozen over, he would catch different kinds of fish by hooking them through holes cut in the ice. He would be permitted to hunt small animals by setting snares, to catch ptarmigans with deadfall traps, and to set fish traps under the ice. And he would take trips with his tutor and observe his techniques in hunting the more dangerous large animals such as wolves and bear.

Masu informed the tutor that she would teach her new son how to make the snares, nets, fishhooks, and traps he would need. She explained further that, although men normally were not expected to learn the woman's simple ways of hunting for small animals, such as the methods she proposed teaching her son, she thought that he would benefit from knowing these things. She added jokingly, "When he first gets married, he'll take pride in bringing home small game animals to his bride."

Laughing, Unaq nodded his head, signifying his approval of her plans. He offered to train Nulthkutuk in the more dangerous methods of hunting.

Masu said to him, "Nulthkutuk will have a new kayak by spring. He is a promising young man, and no doubt it will not be too difficult for him to paddle his kayak since he has had considerable training already in how to paddle the canoe of his own people. Learning through experience is the best way. When our skilled craftsmen are at work, especially constructing an umiak or kayak and other major items, be sure Nulthkutuk is permitted to observe them, Unaq."

Unag promised her he would make arrangements with the craftsmen in the village to fulfill her wishes. Then he suggested to her that Nulthkutuk must attend all recreational and educational functions and celebrations which were offered to the citizens at the *kargi*, or council house.

She was pleased by his suggestion, for to her it was an important part of her son's education to learn their folklore with its beautiful theme songs, legends, philosophical dogmas, beliefs, myths, interpretative dancing, singing, and interesting historical tales which the old sages had handed down to the young folks as patterns of behavior.

Masu extended her gratitude to Unaq by shaking his hand.

Unaq smiled and said to her, "It gives me great pleasure to accept your offer of the position of tutor. Tomorrow morning my assistant, Qunigrak, and I will go over these plans and in the afternoon I'll send him over to your igloo to meet your son.

Let them get acquainted first, before they go out to play with the other children."

"*Ah* [yes]. *Quyahnaa* [thank you], Unaq. The beginning of our responsibility of training the future young chief begins tomorrow. Shall we present our plans to our chief before you go home? You and he will have to decide how you may wish to be paid for your services," Masu suggested.

"Of course. Thank you for reminding me," answered Unaq.

Masu and Unaq entered the great chief's igloo. Masu explained to him why they had come. She then left them to decide on Unaq's payment.

When she entered her porch, she noticed that her son had done all the chores which she was accustomed to doing every day. She thought to herself that it was a pleasant culmination to all the uncertainties she had gone through the past week. It was comforting to know that in the future there would be one to share her home life, love, and the happiness and sorrows to come in their efforts to gain a livelihood. Her son would have to grow physically and mentally and, above all, she hoped that he would accept the leadership of her people.

When she came into the igloo, she smiled, then she knew that she was happier than ever before. Soon, her son would communicate naturally with her.

Masu went to bed. Though sleepless at first, she was enjoying the images flashing in her mind, pictures of her son's future life. Then she fell asleep.

When she awoke the next morning, she revisualized the orderly imagery that had appeared to her the night before, and matched it with her son's educational schedule, to begin that very morning.

It was the beginning of Nulthkutuk's training to be chief, a time which Masu knew would pass too quickly. First there would be the childhood days, then adolescence, and finally the last phase of training before manhood. Masu smiled as she thought of her son's first successful homecoming from hunting the *ugruk* [bearded seal]. Could he actually learn to become such a skilled hunter by the time of coming of age?

Almost as quickly as the passage of Masu's thoughts, Nulthkutuk was a young man. By the time he was twenty he had passed all his tests and prepared to become a full-fledged, skillful, and crafty hunter.

One evening in the last years of his training, his former tutor, now counselor, advised him that in the morning he must try his skill in hunting the big game, the *ugruk*, an animal only the expert hunter can catch. He felt honored to be chosen for such a task. If he were successful, it would be a sign of his maturity to all the people. He ran home to his mother to tell the good news and to ask her to prepare his hunting equipment. He went to bed early after he invited his companion to join him the next day.

He and his companion, Qunigrak, left with the dog team for the home of the *ugruk*, near the edge of the thin, moving ice by the sea. Their counselor's last advice had been to sit quietly away from the edge and listen patiently for the breathing sounds of the animal.

Before daylight, they approached their destination. They left their team and walked the rest of the way to the edge of the old ice where they settled down to watch and listen for the bearded seal.

As they were sitting several feet apart, a huge *ugruk* appeared through the thin ice to take a breath. As he did, Nulthkutuk noticed he was facing the edge of the ice. He made motions to Qunigrak indicating that he would kill the animal after it went to sleep. Qunigrak understood. They watched while the *ugruk* noisily clawed its way up on the ice, where finally it went to sleep. They waited a long while before Nulthkutuk began to stalk closer to the animal, inch by inch. While the young hunter was crawling toward the animal, the *ugruk* was awakened, but did not plunge back into the water. At last Nulthkutuk was near enough to thrust his spear; as he did, the huge animal heaved around in circles. Both men ran to the helpless *ugruk*. Nulthkutuk stabbed it again with his long-bladed spear, and held it there until the victim succumbed. Both men were so overwhelmed with joy that they yelled loudly. At that moment their dogs echoed them, answering the announcement of the successful catch.

"Now we must dress the animal," Nulthkutuk reminded his companion.

"No! No!" objected Qunigrak, "We must not do such a thing. Remember the custom. We will haul the animal as it is to the village. And before we leave the ice we will give it water to withdraw its spirit from the flesh."

Nulthkutuk thanked his companion, and ran to get the dog team.

# 4
# NULTHKUTUK BECOMES CHIEF

THE ASCENDANCY of the future chief became evident to the people when they heard that Nulthkutuk had successfully bagged an ugruk. They knew that there would be a traditional feast, a commemoration of his manhood, at which time he and his mother would give gifts to the honored guests, the aged people of Unalakleet, as a symbol of acknowledgment. Furthermore, on this occasion Nulthkutuk would offer some food to the girl he would choose as his future bride, the customary rite of announcing his engagement to his people. The ceremonial feast would follow the gift-giving.

The time for the feast arrived and, by tradition, the future bride sat with her father and her fiancé's mother. While singers sang a love song, the prospective groom walked slowly toward the family group, carrying a dish filled with such delicacies as ugruk meat, roots, berries, and other food and laid the dish in front of them on a grass mat. The girl Nulthkutuk chose was Aligak, the chief's daughter. If the girl took part of the food and ate, it meant that she accepted his proposal. The well-wishers roared their approval as they watched her eat. Then the young man sat down to eat with the group and the rest of the people joined in.

After the feast, Nulthkutuk and his chosen bride led the ceremonial dance while the villagers looked on. Following that, the chief's family watched different interpretative dances, a comical dance performed by a minstrel, and heard a new song. Another interpretative dance, the highlight of them all, terminated the program.

The hunting dance was usually performed by the successful and brave hunters. They composed the themes song of the drama in which the hunt was reenacted to the people. This performance of the young men became the source of a new song and a dance which would be preserved after the singers learned the song thoroughly. These special songs became a regular part of the features at future ceremonies. Therefore, during the presentation the young hunters performed several times for the singers until the old chief announced the termination.

The main purpose of the celebration was to fulfill a threefold traditional custom: to proclaim the maturity of young men as eligible hunters; to announce engagements of the marriageable young men; and to make known to the people the beginning of training for marriage.

If the new hunter were the son of a chief, he automatically became a member of the council, and for a whole year he was permitted to observe and familiarize himself with the methods by which decisions were defined and rendered. He was taught the techniques of warfare and all the customs of the Eskimo people. At the end of this time, when he had successfully passed his test, he proudly related his experiences to his future bride and mother.

Aligak and Nulthkutuk gave their vows to become rulers of the village, as husband and wife. Aligak was not idle during her year of training. She was taught by her Aunt Masu and the other older women how to do the many household duties of a wife. The following course of study was offered to her: sewing skins, including specialized techniques, cutting seals, making seal pokes, and learning to preserve food. The most difficult test would be making waterproof garments which were used by the hunters and food gatherers. Time after time she failed, but one day Aligak passed her test, and she proudly made a gift set for her aged father.

On the very day of presentation, he adorned himself with his new garments and offered to take his daughter for a kayak ride. Aligak was delighted, but sorrow overwhelmed the old chief. She led him down to the kayak and climbed in facing the stern, her father took his place in the kayak and he began to paddle away from the shore. He took her as far as her mother's grave, laid his paddle across the kayak and rested for a while. The chief could not see the tears that were flowing gently down her cheeks. As the kayak was rolling over the waves, they could hear the rhythmic music of the surf and she compared the span of life and death to the billows yielding their last roll against the beach.

Her father, breaking into her thoughts, said to her, "Bring me here by your mother's grave when the day announces my death, Aligak."

He turned his kayak around and paddled toward the village, over the sunlit, rose-tinted, glossy sea. When they arrived at the village, they carried the kayak by the ends and laid it on its berth.

While they were walking home, he requested that she invite her Aunt Masu and his own namesake, Nulthkutuk, for dinner. Aligak immediately went over to convey the invitation, then she prepared her father's favorite food, Eskimo ice cream, for dessert, and set the table before her guests arrived.

After the dinner, the old chief praised his daughter for the delicious meal. If Aligak had known what the future held for her, she would have understood her father's unusual behavior and requests. However, she did not interpret them until she found him sleeping beyond his usual time the following morning. Not wishing to disturb him, she went over to her aunt's igloo to ask her to wake him up, but before she entered, Masu came out to meet her. Masu knew right away what had happened.

"Come, Auntie, to our igloo and let us both awaken my father." When they went to him, they found he had died in the night. Although Aligak was old enough to stand the shock, she welcomed her aunt's presence at the crisis and wept freely in her arms. Nulthkutuk came. He, too, wept in silence for the chief who had saved his life when Masu had rescued him from the field of battle years ago.

"Son, take the family staff on the roof of our igloo and place it in an upright position first, then tilt it toward the cemetery." Masu remembered how to carry out the required rituals of the burial.

The death of the great chief was announced throughout the village, and the mourning began which continued until several days after the burial.

The old chief was buried with pomp and style with the traditional chieftain's rites. Thereafter, his successor, Masu, was allowed to move into the chief's house to join Aligak, who had been left alone.

When the customary period of mourning was over, Nulthkutuk and his bride had a simple wedding in the *kargii* (council house), and all the people of the village were invited to the ceremony. The eldest sage of the council officiated at the wedding. The groom sat with the sage and his mother as the bride offered food to her future husband while the wedding song was being sung. Nulthkutuk extended his hand to her, which was the recognized gesture of acceptance. The old sage announced their marriage and the feast followed. After the feast the couple received their gifts as the people left for their homes. Under normal circumstances, the guests would dance all night at a wedding, but at the wedding of Nulthkutuk and Aligak, Masu requested they postpone the merrymaking until the loss of the chief was obliterated.

After the wedding ceremony, Masu planned an outing for Aligak with several other experienced food gatherers. She explained to them that perhaps if they invited the girl to go out berry picking, digging roots and fishing with them, she would gradually return to her normal self. Masu told them that it was too hard for her to carry the burden alone. The women were willing to undertake the outing she suggested.

Aligak's training in identifying edible vegetables eased her grief and the fall and winter months swiftly passed.

Spring offered many more activities for the food gatherers. Although Aligak was expecting her first baby, she was not allowed to remain idle. When the couple were alone, they would plan together activities for their baby. They were pleased to hear that Masu had agreed to train the child for them.

Late one evening Masu was summoned and Aligak announced that the labor pains had begun. According to custom, Aligak was taken out to a little hut to follow instructions from Masu, who had taken a place outside the hut. When the baby was born, Masu attended and cared for the baby. Aligak and the child were required to stay in their hut alone until purification had taken place, when the umbilical cord had healed and both had been cleaned according to ritual. The mother was then allowed to return to her igloo with her baby, to be with her husband and people. The baby was named after Nulthkutuk's real father, Maktak, with Masu's approval. And as he held his baby during the naming ceremony, he noticed that the child's features were similar to his father's. Nulthkutuk could not control his emotion, and he allowed the tears to roll down his cheeks. His wife thought his tears were tears of joy, but in fact they were from homesickness. The young father prayed to the Ruler of the Universe that he and his baby might one day meet their relatives who lived in the Interior, near the Yukon River.

The people of Unalakleet were proud of the infant, their future chief, and the old sages predicted that Nulthkutuk's wife would bear more sons. Thereafter, every other year a new child was born and within ten years, they had four boys and one daughter. Both Aligak and Masu reared the children, and the chief, Nulthkutuk, was grateful to his aged foster mother for the love and help she gave his family through the years.

He said to his wife one day, "My mother is not spry anymore and she looks tired. I wonder if she would like to move into her own house where it is quieter?" Aligak approved of the idea, as did Masu.

Masu moved several weeks later, and one of her grandchildren lived with her. Nulthkutuk and his family visited her frequently. They enjoyed the historical tales she told, especially about the Eskimo and Indian wars.

One evening she made him promise never to desert his family and his rightful role as chief. He promised her that he would defend his people, and told her of his plans for strengthening his warriors.

"I will call my warriors to a meeting tonight." Before the meeting he sent for his personal aide to plan the agenda. One of his purposes in calling the meeting was to clarify the actions of his warriors during an attack.

When they met, he called on the council to give a report about the condition of the equipment, and other leaders reported to him that they would repair the *umiaks*.

"See that all the paddles are in the boats ready for action," he ordered. The closing command he gave during his speech was that no one should leave the igloos until he gave a signal. Then he explained to them that he had felt insecure lately, and that in case of emergency, he wanted them to be ready to face the foe with strength and unity. The meeting adjourned. As soon as he entered his igloo he was confronted with bad news.

Nulthkutuk was not surprised when his wife told him that his mother had passed away, and despite his grief he remembered to announce her death to the people by tilting his staff toward the cemetery, the customary indication of death in a family.

He and his people mourned for his mother, Queen Masu. They went through the traditional burial rites. Nulthkutuk knew he would miss the guidance of his mother, her cheerfulness, and her help in bearing the responsibility for their safety in times of crisis.

The protection of his people in the event of another Indian raid remained in his mind since his mother's death. During the sleepless nights he thoroughly reviewed his part—a role he would fulfil bravely to show his loyalty to the people, the Eskimos, who through Masu had saved him from starvation.

The actual time of testing arrived late one evening while the chief and his men were in the council house. A messenger conveyed a secret message to his chief announcing that the village was already surrounded by Indian warriors who evidently planned to burn their igloos with torches. Nulthkutuk took his megaphone and dashed out, climbed the roof of the council house, and faced the foe.

As he stood at the center of the igloo, he began to relate the history and outcome of the last battle between the two tribes.

They listened to him instead of attacking his people. He then related the aftermath of the battle, and told how the chief's sister had saved him from starvation and suffering probable death from exposure.

His last message to the Indian warriors, once his own people, was a brave challenge and a request. "Unalakleet Eskimos are my people now; I am their chief, and to become eligible for the position of chief, I married the old chief's daughter and when his sister, the queen, my foster mother, died, I became their chief. I have four sons and a daughter.

"My challenge to you, my Indian relatives, is this: If you wish to annihilate my people the Eskimos, I request that you kill me first, for I cannot witness the suffering of the people who saved my life."

There was no answer, but later he watched his Indian relatives and one-time enemies paddling their canoes up the Unalakleet River—to him a clear sign of retreat.

In the morning, while his people were sleeping, the chief, savior of the Unalakleet people, walked down to the beach and found a, message for him—a request for a friendly reunion, at which time Nulthkutuk would see his true relatives for the first time since he was a little lost boy.

This is the legend of Alluyagnak I and Alluyagnak II, my distant ancestors, and the beginnings of the Unalakleet people as handed down orally from generation to generation. What follow are of a more recent time and are the recollections of people who told these things to me.

# II

# MALQUAY

# 5
# MALQUAY'S YOUTH

"MOTHER, TAKE my baby and pack her on your back," Qunigrak asked his mother, as he turned the *umiak* toward the shore for landing. Baby Malquay cried when she was pulled from her mother's breast. It was her last contact with her mother, for her mother had just died. In years to come, Malquay had no recollection of her mother except that day when she had her last milk from her.

Qunigrak and his mother prepared their loved one for burial, following the customary rituals. After the burial, Qunigrak and his remaining family set sail toward Unalakleet village, traveling near the coastline of Norton Sound. He could hear the breakers on the seashore and their sound consoled him in his loss. He sang a parting song to his wife, a song of grief, mingled with the rhythmic tempo of the ocean beating the shore that he followed closely in his *umiak*. The midnight sun extended its rays from the horizon across the rolling waves as if to cheer him.

His mother, who was named Masu after the first Masu, offered him some food, which he refused. But the thought of home eased his pain as they approached the village.

When they arrived, it was wonderful to be with his relatives, the chief, and his family. Gradually, Qunigrak regained his composure as he settled again among his own people. His dead wife's brother, Uyagak Rock, and his cousins (the chief and his brothers) welcomed him and selected a place where he could build an igloo near the chief's yard.

But in spite of all they did, his life was not the same; he was lonely. Furthermore, because his mother was really too old to take care of his two little daughters, he decided to seek a second wife. One morning he revealed these plans to his mother. Before he left, she advised him not to settle too far away from Unalakleet. He promised her that he had no intention of traveling farther than Shaktoolik, about forty miles up the coast, and that he would come back within a year or two.

Qunigrak felt that separations of family ties were crucial experiences, especially for a man with a motherless family, because there could never be a complete separation when children are involved. Love, sustenance, anxiety about their health, and the responsibility of being both father and mother to the girls were some of the problems he felt instinctively.

His mother sensed that her son was leaving for an extended stay, so she asked him for the legal custody of her grandchildren, Malquay and Amak. He gave his consent with the understanding that he be permitted to support them. Once again, baby Malquay was parted from a parent. She was almost two years old when her father left them, and she retained no clear recollection of him.

Several years had elapsed when one day he returned with his second wife and a new baby. Their stepmother tried repeatedly to persuade the girls to move to their father's home, but she was unsuccessful. The girls stayed with their grandmother.

More and more, they were deprived of the necessities of life. Although Qunigrak encouraged his wife to supply his mother and his daughters with food and skins for clothing, she intentionally ignored his wishes. Many times he brought his catch directly to his mother instead of to his wife. His wife became very jealous of Qunigrak's attitude toward his daughters. Therefore, the girls lived as semi-orphans during their early childhood with their grandmother.

The older daughter, Amak, was her father's favorite and Malquay was loved very dearly by her grandmother. Amak had access to the prettiest fur clothing, while Malquay had to be satisfied with her sister's old clothing. Amak, therefore, was reared with a feeling of superiority over her younger sister. Many times Malquay had to be pacified by her grandmother to make up for Amak's mistreatment.

One evening after supper, Amak made fun of her sister, called her names, and even went so far as to turn Malquay's nose up with her index finger. Her grandmother said to her, "Amak, do not mistreat your little sister. Some day when you both grow up, you will want something from Malquay, for I know she will have a fine home."

"Haha! Do you think this girl will have anything worthwhile that I could want?" Amak laughed again, as she pointed to her sister.

Their grandmother, Masu, said to them, "Hurry and get ready for bed, and I will tell you stories." Malquay enjoyed listening to folklore; she remembered the stories and songs just as her grandmother told them to her. This folklore became a lasting part of her life.

In due time, she was old enough to visit at her neighbors next door. As most children will, one day she stayed too long. Consequently, her grandmother had to go out to seek Malquay when it was bedtime. After she went to bed, she began to cry.

"Why are you crying?" asked her grandmother.

"My cousin had pancakes this evening and she didn't give me any—and pancakes are very good, Grandmother," sobbed Malquay. Now, her grandmother knew that flour had just been introduced to the village, but it was very expensive and only the chief's family had any. However, she wished to comfort her dear little Malquay, and she said, "Listen, Malquay, some day when you become a lady, you will have lots of flour in your home and you can make pancakes every day." And thus Malquay was comforted.

They were fortunate to be living next door to the chief's family and, because her grandmother was the chief's sister, they were treated well.

One day, the grandmother announced to the girls that they were leaving for St. Michael. Amak began dancing around the tent, clapping her hands.

"*Arig'a! Ariga!* Malquay, *ami?*" (Fine! Fine! All right, Malquay?] Malquay had not traveled anywhere since her mother's death, therefore she had no reason to be happy over traveling to this place called St. Michael (Tusiq). But Amak had gone there once with her father, and she remembered they bought strange food called *asiakpanjit* (big berries, or oranges and apples).

"Why are you glad, Amak?" Malquay asked her sister.

"Sit down, you stupid girl! I will tell you about this big place." So she told her about the big, big city where different types of people lived in tall igloos. She told Malquay about the big berries (apples and oranges) there, which were as big as the skin balls with which the village children played.

Malquay sat listening attentively with her big eyes rolling around. Puzzled, she was trying to picture in her mind the appearance of these strange white people, when the sisters suddenly heard their grandmother speaking, "Hurry up, girls! Pack your things, we are leaving soon. Be sure to put your boots on, and warm parkas. It will be cold."

# 6

# MALQUAY'S FIRST VISIT TO ST. MICHAEL

DURING THE latter part of May on the coast of Norton Sound, the Eskimos are usually set free from the hard grip of the wintry blast. It is a time for hunting at their spring camps away from their communities. As soon as the shore ice drifts away, families leave their camps to visit their friends and relatives who live in neighboring villages on the coast.

Late one evening, Qunigrak decided to take his mother and his girls, Amak and Malquay, for a short vacation to St. Michael. They set off, sailing in his *umiak* near the shore until they came to the cliffs, then Qunigrak changed his course directly toward the peninsula called Nuggak, about midway between their spring camp and St. Michael. He advised his mother to put the girls to bed. Amak, the older daughter, as usual, did not like the idea of being forced to bed, but a compromise with her father ended her opposition and she accepted the challenge. "Amak, do you see that long, narrow land out in the sea?" She nodded. "We'll be there early in the morning. If you go to bed in the bow now, I promise that you and your little sister can gather wild duck eggs on a beautiful island tomorrow morning."

Amak gave him a big smile and ducked inside the sleeping bag. Qunigrak felt relieved when the girls finally went to sleep.

He thought of his uncle who had left with his family to go to St. Michael earlier in the day. Qunigrak himself preferred the time just before sunset as the ideal time for traveling in an open boat. He liked to take his time and enjoy the beautiful scenery. Usually at that time the wind moderates enough to allow the *umiak* to travel at a favorable speed. Moreover, beluga [white whale] hunting could be possible on the way. To him, sailing was a means of relaxation, a complete break from his innumerable daily concerns. It was a time for welcoming migratory birds and sea mammals such as the whale, to enjoy the beautiful rays of many colors reflected by the midnight sun, and to breathe the aroma of the vegetation from the land. Above all, he was grateful to his aged mother who was rearing his girls, teaching them the traditional way of life. She, too, must be enjoying the evening glow of golden yellow sunset, part of which was flashing on the sail of his *umiak* as it bobbed up and down over the rolling waves.

Although his mother had offered to relieve him from the task of steering the *umiak*, he did not wish to move from his comfortable position. Instead, he asked her if she would like to accompany the girls on the egg hunt at the island. She answered that they might gather enough eggs for breakfast.

Soon after, the sun set, but Qunigrak knew that it would rise again in a short time. The wind began to blow more gustily and since they were approaching the point, Nuggak, he decided to steer the *umiak* to the lee side of the peninsula. As they were skirting around the seashore they saw many cliff birds flying back and forth, challenging the intruders. Masu noticed that the ptarmigan willow leaves had fully grown. 'I will pick fresh green willow leaves for our lunch this morning," she turned and announced to her son.

The other side of the peninsula was calm, so Qunigrak towed the *umiak* toward an inlet. He noticed that the sun had appeared above the horizon over the distant rugged mountains. The essence of the spring awakening and the warmth in the air was invigorating. He took his family to the center of the inlet and pulled the *umiak* onto the beach. They would rest in this sheltered place before they set sail again for St. Michael in the evening.

Qunigrak carried a basket of food to a spot where they would eat their breakfast. He gathered some driftwood and built a fire, while his mother searched for water. When she came back, she suspended the tea pot over the flames on the tip of a narrow willow pole, which was made firmly fast in the ground. Qunigrak carried the sleepy girls one by one and laid them on a caribou skin in front of the grass mat on which the food was set for breakfast.

Both girls now came wide awake as their father was presenting his plans for the day. Their grandmother asked them if they would like to hunt for duck eggs after breakfast. By this time, both were thoroughly aroused and, to her astonishment, they began walking away, presumably to search for the duck eggs. Qunigrak and his mother laughed and called them back to eat their breakfast.

While they were doing so, Qunigrak pointed toward the sea and exclaimed, "Whales! They are heading right for the cove. Mother, I will try to harpoon one."

He ran quickly down to the *umiak* to arrange his weapons. Then he ran back to his family and ordered the girls to hide in the willows immediately. At the same time, he told his mother that she could help him to maneuver the *umiak*. He quickly smothered the flames of the campfire with wet moss. Then he and his mother towed the *umiak* to a jetty on the peninsula, there to wait for the best time to attack. The whales came directly to the cove to drink fresh water and their course took them in the direction of the jetty. As they came up for a breath of air, their gleaming white bodies curved above the surface of the sea. Qunigrak ducked inside the *umiak*, ready to rise and thrust his harpoon at the nearest whale. In a moment he was alongside the whale. The time to hurl the harpoon was—now! Suddenly there appeared before them a great upheaval of sea water and spray and in an instant the whale sounded.

Qunigrak let go of the heavy line and threw it out on the water where it would unwind itself as they were being pulled by the harpooned whale. Qunigrak was glad when he saw the inflated seal poke buoy floating over the captive whale. Whenever the line slackened, he skillfully rewound it, little by little, around the shuttle which was attached to the side of the *umiak*. The beluga continued to pull them, however, as Qunigrak hauled in the line, bringing the *umiak* closer and closer to the whale.

This part of the chase is the most dangerous part of whale hunting, especially in an open boat. Sometimes an *umiak* will capsize if the sea is stormy. Only experts may manipulate the towline.

When he was close enough, Qunigrak thrust the double-bladed harpoon deep into the side of the whale. After a short struggle for life, the mammal died and its body began to float. Qunigrak and his mother tied the flippers firmly to the side of the *umiak* and then its tail, until the whale lay awash on the surface of the water. It took them quite a while to reach the shore, for the north wind was bucking against their skin boat. When they arrived on the beach, the girls told them they were hungry for *muktuk*, the whale's outer skin, which is a delicacy.

For the rest of the morning, it was evident that the whole family would have to make preparations for butchering the catch, but not until all had eaten their leftover breakfast. While they were eating, Qunigrak discussed with his mother whether or not they should take some *muktuk* to St. Michael. Masu encouraged him to take most of it to share with the people. So before their departure, they butchered the beluga whale, taking off the *muktuk* in blocks. As they took off each block, they laid it in the large skin container which was in the middle of the boat. The choicest cuts of meat were loaded next. Then they buried the rest of the whale in a deep hole in the ground lined with dry hay, and covered the meat with hay and a thick layer of topsoil. They would retrieve it on their way back home from St. Michael.

When Qunigrak finished this task, he asked his mother if she would accompany the girls to hunt for eggs while he rested before sailing. The girls were thrilled when she agreed to go.

Masu allowed the girls to gather some game bird eggs and sea duck eggs, but before they did, she taught them the rule which parents were obligated to pass on to the next generation. She went with them to the first nest of eider duck eggs and explained that they were not to take all the eggs.

"Why, grandmother?" Amak, the older girl, asked. "I want to pick all of them."

The old woman explained to them that if they took all the eggs, in the future there would not be any more birds. They would become extinct. The second lesson she taught them was how to test if the eggs had developed into little birds. She demonstrated this by taking one egg from the nest and submerging it in a pool of water. The egg sank all the way to the bottom of the pool. She explained that the egg had not as yet formed into a little bird. They went back to the nest and she took only half of the eight eider duck eggs. She also told them they should not handle the rest of the eggs, since if they did, the mother would not sit on them because she could scent the human odor on the eggs, which would be very offensive to her. When Malquay found a nest of eggs she performed the same experiment her grandmother had previously. Masu allowed her to pick up the egg and carry it to the same pool to test it, and when she dropped the egg in the water, it floated. Then their grandmother asked Amak why it floated on the surface. The girl answered that there was a little bird in the egg. And Masu said no one likes to eat little birds and that it was better for them to become big birds instead. Both girls nodded their heads in agreement.

When they had filled their wooden buckets, they went back to where their father was sleeping. Masu said they would have some cooked *muktuk* and eggs for supper. Amak asked her grandmother if she could boil the eggs, and then she turned to her younger sister and told her to gather wood and get some water for them. Malquay knew it was an order that she would have to obey, so she consented to do the work for her big sister. He grandmother put her arm around Malquay while they walked over to the boat.

Masu told the girls not to wake their father until the food was cooked and supper was ready. She called to the girls and suggested that they pick some ptarmigan willow leaves, just enough for their father. While they were picking leaves, she cooled the meat and the *muktuk* that she had boiled. Within a short while the girls came from picking leaves, so she asked Amak to wake her father. When they sat down to eat, Amak laughed and told her father how they helped their grandmother.

"Mother, I hope you'll teach my little girl, Ozuk, the interpretative dancing." Masu promised him she would teach her soon. When Qunigrak used Ozuk as Malquay's pet name, he did so because she was so dear to him. Such a pet name is given to a member of a family who is born shortly after the death of another.

After supper, he took his daughters for a short walk up to the highest knoll. He told his mother that he must observe the sky to see what the weather would be before they left that night. While he studied the sky for signs of bad weather, the girls picked winter cranberries. He was glad when his observations indicated that the wind would not blow too hard and he told his mother that the weather was favorable when they returned to the cove.

They set sail, and the offshore wind sent them quickly toward their destination. Masu sang her Eskimo lullabies to her grandchildren until they both went to sleep. And before she went to sleep she composed a theme song which Malquay would use with her interpretative dance during the next midwinter festival. She sang it over and over again until she knew it by heart.

As Qunigrak sailed on and on, he watched the migratory birds far and near. He considered the snares he had stored in his *umiak* and thought that perhaps on their homeward trip he would hunt for ducks.

Soon Qunigrak would sight St. Michael, so he suggested that his mother take a nap before they arrived at the white men's village.

By early morning, Qunigrak had to take his mind off the waterfowl and concentrate on beaching the *umiak*, for he was approaching St. Michael's shore. As he sailed his skin boat closer to the land, he saw a white line near the beach. This was shore ice which might block his beaching. When he stood up and examined the outside edge of the ice, he saw a wide crack in it. As he approached the crack, he noticed that the space was wide enough to permit him to paddle his way through. While he was paddling, he examined the high palisade which lay before him. Beneath this bank on the dry beach there were many tents, so aligned that the reflection from the ice had prevented him from seeing them earlier. Perhaps his cousin's tent would be here. He knew his cousin, the Unalakleet chief, Delialuk, would invite them all to be his guest since they had come only for a visit.

As much as he would have liked to show St. Michael to Malquay immediately, he felt that he should pitch his tent first and get settled.

Qunigrak beached his *umiak*; he was not surprised to see his cousin waiting on the shore to welcome him.

"You came early this time, Qunigrak. You and your family will be our guests until we all leave for Unalakleet in a few days."

Qunigrak accepted this invitation gladly, and he began to unload his *umiak*. The chief then led the way to his tent. Qunigrak carried the still-sleeping Malquay and laid her on Delialuk's wife's bed. Masu followed with Amak who, although barely awake, carried a bucket full of fresh duck eggs neatly embedded in soft moss. She announced proudly to Delialuk, as she handed the bucket to him, "Malquay and I gathered these eggs for you and Tatgavin yesterday." Maktak thanked her and asked his wife to boil the eggs for his breakfast. Amak smiled from ear to ear as she sat down beside him.

Masu and her son related their experiences en route to St. Michael from Unalakleet, then Qunigrak excused himself to haul their personal effects to his host's tent. He would set up his own tent later. On his last trip to the boat, he brought the leftover supply of cooked *muktuk* and laid this in front of Delialuk's wife, Tatgavin. His cousins were surprised that he had successfully bagged a beluga whale.

While they were eating breakfast, little Malquay awoke and sat up facing them, blinking and rubbing her eyes in confusion. When she saw her grandmother, she went to her. The chief urged his wife to give the girls some pilot bread. Malquay's curiosity was intensely aroused as she held the disk of pilot bread in her little hands. Her grandmother explained to her that it was *naluaqmite's* (people of the bleached sealskin, or white men) bread, not a toy. She glanced at her sister, Amak, and listened to the crackling sound as she munched on the hardtack. Malquay gave the hard bread to her grandmother and asked her to put it in her bag. Masu gave her boiled egg and *muktuk* to eat instead.

Delialuk and his wife were amused at Malquay's first reaction to the white man's food. Her great-aunt, Tatgavin, said, "Just wait and see how she will react to the *naluaqmite's asiakpanjit* [white man's big berries - oranges and apples]."

After breakfast, Amak took her little sister for a walk on the beach beneath the 30-foot embankment. They walked past many Eskimo tents in line along the low seashore. Beyond this row of tents they saw many large and small boats anchored near the pier. It was all new and interesting to them and when they approached the scene of activity, Amak sat on a flat-topped boulder and invited her wide-eyed little sister to sit by her side.

They watched many people walking on a wooden boardwalk built over and above the high bank. It was a fascinating spectacle to watch the many races of people dressed in different types of clothing coming and going. Their grandmother attempted to persuade them several times to go back to the tent with her, but failing, she too then sat and watched the march of these newcomers to their land.

# 7

# MALQUAY ENCOUNTERS A STRANGE CULTURE

Tatgavin prepared the food for her guests and laid it on a grass mat outdoors near their tent before she searched for them. She climbed onto the high bank by the seashore in order to quickly identify her guests from among the crowd. She saw her husband and Qunigrak walking home from the Eskimo village where they had visited the chief of the St. Michael Eskimos, and also quickly spotted Masu and her grandchildren watching the longshoremen unload cargo from the Yukon River sternwheeler which was tied to the pier. She noticed several other steamships anchored out in the sea near the edge of the onshore ice, probably waiting for the ice to drift away. On the seashore, people were milling back and forth about the pier. She did not realize that many of these strange men were en route to Nome, Council, Kobuk, and Fairbanks to seek gold. She did not know that they had come from the United States and other countries.

All around and above her were many kinds of birds, some passing through on their migration to the north. It was good to listen to the noisy crows, seagulls, and melodious songbirds. As she stood there, she had pleasant recollections of the happy times of her childhood. She pictured herself running around with the butterflies here and there, and how she would sit listening to her grandmother's crow stories. Crows were always comical birds in the stories, and it was against the custom to kill them.

Tatgavin stood for a while enraptured by Nature's wonder-land before she continued with her search. Then she realized that she must leave her perch and walk down the bank to join Masu and the children. When she announced that lunch was ready, the girls didn't want to leave such an interesting place. Tatgavin casually told their grandmother that perhaps after lunch they could all go to the town and see other interesting places. The girls beamed with excitement and went with their great-aunt to the tent.

They were glad to see their father, as usual, and when they sat down to eat, Amak did most of the talking about what they had seen. But her father was also curious to hear Malquay give her account of her experiences. He knew that she would not speak unless he encouraged her.

"Malquay, tell us about your good times."

She smiled shyly before she spoke. "I saw many strangers on the pier. They had many things to carry on their backs. These *naluaqmite* sounded like a group of hungry, yelping seagulls, and like seagulls were trying to get some of the discarded garbage."

When her relatives laughed at her comparison, she ducked behind her father, since she seldom drew people's attention. Her father embraced his youngest daughter until her composure was restored. Amak, of course, continued to laugh until her grandmother quieted her.

Tatgavin reminded the girls of her plans—that soon after lunch they would visit the beautiful building the whites called the Russian Orthodox church. This would be another new experience for Masu and her grandchildren, for they were not familiar with the different types of white men's igloos, such as barracks, stores, post offices and churches.

When they had finished eating, Masu urged the girls to wash, then she changed their parkas and her own. Before they all departed, Delialuk invited them to a feast and Eskimo dance at the village that evening and so he urged them to come home early.

Masu announced her plans also. Malquay would have a chance to practice her sailing interpretative dance. She glanced over at Amak and said, "Amak will dance the salmonberry-picking interpretative dance." Masu excused the girls and told them to wash their hands. She gave them each a handmade shredded-grass towel, such as Eskimos had used many generations ago. She combed their hair with an ivory comb. They said goodbyes to Delialuk and Qunigrak and departed, Tatgavin leading the way.

While they were walking up the broad wooden sidewalk they heard a small bell ringing for the first time. Tatgavin stopped and pointed in the direction of the sound. They saw the beautiful big igloo which was located on a peninsula just across the cove.

Tatgavin suggested that they walk over to see it more closely. The bell was bobbing up and down inside the mushroom-shaped tower. Many strangely dressed people, evidently going to the same place, passed by. Amak was brave and interested, but Malquay clung to Masu's side, while Tatgavin uttered comforting words to her. "*Iksi nai chute* [they won't hurt you], Malquay.

Many people entered the church as they came into the churchyard. Tatgavin led the little girls to the side of the wooden walk and the four of them sat down to watch the procession. The girls were fascinated by the people's strange garments, and by the fact that as the strangers walked, their shoes squeaked. Tatgavin was waiting for Malquay's reaction to the sound of the squeaky shoes. The little girl looked at her own boots and said to Masu, "Grandmother, I am glad my *gamaka* [boots] don't squeak."

Among the last group of people there appeared a young boy who was walking with an older white man. Malquay observed his stature, the way he wore his straw hat and how his shoes squeaked, before he disappeared into the beautiful white and red igloo. She thought, "I hope we can visit the inside of the church; I'd like to see that boy again." Her wish would come true one day. Not only would she see him again, but she would marry him.

Tatgavin asked Masu and the girls if they would like to go to the big town of St. Michael. They all wanted to see the town, so they left the churchyard. Amak and Malquay walked happily on the wooden sidewalk beside Tatgavin. When they had come close enough to the center of town, Masu suggested to Tatgavin that they watch the people from where they were. So they sat down again, this time to examine a series of box-like igloos built in straight rows.

Masu was deeply impressed with such buildings, and finally her curiosity was aroused to the point that she asked Tatgavin if many people lived in those houses.

Tatgavin nodded.

The buildings were the barracks of the United States Army. Masu pointed to the flagpole and asked the girls if they noticed the beautiful flag which was hoisted to the tip of the pole. None of the group knew why the colorful cloth was flying there.

# 8
# HOMEWARD BOUND

QUNISRAK'S FAMILY enjoyed their visit to St. Michael and with Delialuk and Tatgavin, but in a few days he became anxious to go home. He announced to his mother and the girls after supper that they would leave early in the morning. A command from their father also sent both girls to bed early. After they had gone to bed, their grandmother helped them to sleep by telling stories from the folklore of their people and singing lullabies. In a little while the girls had fallen fast asleep.

Masu then began to pack their belongings so her son could load them before breakfast. She must not forget to place their food, hunting equipment, and survival items near at hand in the boat. After she and her son had packed their things, Delialuk and his wife also decided to leave that same day. He announced his plans to his guests. "Since we will have a heavy load, I am wondering if you would take part of my personal effects with you tomorrow."

Qunigrak answered him obligingly, offering to lighten his load. "We will need ballast anyway in case the sea suddenly becomes rough. We will be very happy to carry your things in our boat.

"I'll help you load your *umiak* in the morning before I set sail. The wind is blowing from the south and before noon we'll reach

Nuggak, where we can have our lunch together. And before we leave for Unalakleet, you and I will be able to hunt for some game birds. I brought my snares along. In fact, I expect I'll have enough time to set a few snares before you reach Nuggak. When we get back to Unalakleet, we'll have fresh ducks and geese for supper, if these women can do the plucking while we are en route to our village. If we leave in the early afternoon, we'll possibly be at home before midnight."

His cousin Delialuk smiled approvingly and expressed his thanks. He then glanced at his wife and nodded to her to commence packing their belongings, but she waited until the men had gone out of the tent before she fetched the waterproof seal pokes, the tanned sealskins used as packing containers. Masu helped, tying the bolo strings securely at the openings of the pokes. With all the preparations for sailing in the morning completed, both women retired before the men came back from their evening walk.

Masu, the oldest member of the group, rose early in the morning. She decided to cook their breakfast out of doors. When the Eskimo tea had been made, she went into the tent, set a grass mat near the chief's bed, and laid out the cold seal meat and boiled blubber. For her grandchildren, she placed white man's pilot bread as a treat. Then she sat down and very quietly announced, "It is time to eat now."

The chief replied, "*Ah* [yes]." Then the rest of the family got up and, after washing up outdoors, came back in and sat around the mat to eat their breakfast.

Malquay sat on her grandmother's lap sleepy-eyed, but began playing with the pilot bread, for it was the second time she had held such a perfectly-rounded disc. Her grandmother urged her to eat and offered the girl some of the seal meat. Malquay gave her pilot bread to her grandmother and said, "I'll eat it while we are traveling in the boat." Her sister, Amak, had become accustomed to the foreign food, so Masu provided extra pilot bread for her.

When they had eaten their breakfast, they did the last-minute chores, then Masu and her grandchildren settled comfortably in their boat and waited for Qunigrak, who was helping his cousin to load his *umiak*. When ready, he pushed his cousin's boat into the sea, and then shoved off in his own *umiak*.

Qunigrak used his paddle to leave the shore because they were in the leeside of the cove where it was protected from the winds and his sail would not have filled. They traveled in this manner until they were well out in Norton Sound, quite a ways from St. Michael. When the wind became favorable, Qunigrak raised his sail and set course for Nuggak, which was visible across the bay.

Qunigrak looked back at the accompanying boat, and as he did, he noticed that Delialuk had also settled down to enjoy the trip. Qunigrak expertly led the way as they sailed leisurely on. He could hear his cousin sing a traditional Eskimo traveling song. He glanced over to his passengers, and he was not surprised to see them sleeping, for they had left much earlier than he had expected. He was thankful they were asleep because the sea was becoming more and more choppy, and they were beginning to travel faster. He estimated they would reach their destination, the island where they had buried the remains of the whale on their voyage south, before the sun stood directly above them. Because his boat was not carrying as heavy a load as Delialuk's, he knew he would be the first one to arrive. So he decided to beach his boat at a spot where he had snared many ducks in the past. In order to save time, he asked his mother to untangle his snares and help set some of them for him.

As they were nearing the island, they were greeted by many kinds of birds. Qunigrak watched their behavior. They appeared to have a sense of insecurity in their flight. The birds would fly past them and then return to their roosting area as if to give warning to others that danger was near at hand. As the *umiak* drew near the shore, many of the birds flew away. Qunigrak and his mother tied the boat securely to the edge of the bank and invited the girls to go along to watch them as they set the snares. He had two types of snares: those made primarily for women and children, and pole snares usually used by men. The woman's snare had a noose adjustment tied to a substantial two-foot stick, one end of which was tapered. This served as an anchor post and was set with another stick to prop it on one side of the duck path, an easily detected trail that usually ran between two lakes. The other type of snare was made of narrow baleen shavings. Eight to ten snares were placed side by side about four or five inches apart, on a long pole. Each snare had a noose adjustment and string tied securely to the pole. This arrangement of snares was generally placed in a wide creek connecting two lakes, with the snares held underneath the pole.

Qunigrak handed the duck-path snares to his mother. He had three pole snares to set. He waded with them in the shallows of the creeks between the two nearby lakes. When the ducks swam between the two lakes, they would be caught in the snares and strangle themselves when they tried to fly.

The hunter had a feeling that he would be successful in bagging quite a number of wild ducks before the afternoon was over. As they were walking back to their *umiak*, Qunigrak's mother suggested that they should move around to the north side of the peninsula instead of the south side where they had camped on their way to St. Michael. She said to Qunigrak, "You'll have much better chance of snaring more ducks if we camp on the other side of Nuggak. We can eat our lunch there, hidden from their sight."

He accepted her suggestion, and while he was paddling around the peninsula, his cousin appeared and followed them until they came to a good place to eat and rest. As they were eating their lunch, the wind began to blow quite forcefully, and the men knew that they would have to postpone their departure for Unalakleet until late evening. In the meantime, Qunigrak announced to Delialuk that he would have to dig up and haul the whale meat to his boat, but that it would not take him very long to do so. He also wanted to check the snares he had set. He suggested to the women that if they would like to pick winter cranberries, they could take their time and pick enough berries for supper. His little girls, Malquay and Amak, were both very excited at the idea, for they loved to pick berries. Malquay suggested with a smile that perhaps Tatgavin could make Eskimo ice cream for them.

Tatgavin answered her lovingly, "I promise you that I will make *atchagluk* (Eskimo ice cream), especially for you, and the rest of us can eat it too." They rubbed their noses together, and of course Amak had to take part in loving too, so she also rubbed her nose with Tatgavin.

Before they left, Qunigrak invited Delialuk to go along with him to get their favorite food.

He announced, "We'll have *muktuk* for supper tonight."

Qunigrak then gave instructions to his mother. "When you see the smoke at our campsite, you and the girls should come back down here."

They parted and the women began to climb up the hill to look for berry patches, while the men paddled their boat along the shore toward the jagged end of the peninsula.

Near the ridge and around the barren landscape Masu and her companions found many winter cranberries and before it was time to go back to the campsite they filled their buckets. While they were resting they saw the *umiak* bounding toward the campsite. So Masu said to her companions, "Let's start walking slowly down now."

While they were descending they saw curly smoke rising upward beyond the top of the embankment near the shore. The little girls were very happy and they chattered like squirrels as they hopped along together.

The chief's wife cautioned them often not to tumble down among the tussocks, for they were walking on a rugged terrace on the slope of the ridge. They walked fast, but avoided the pitfalls of the tussocks.

When they reached camp, their lunch of *muktuk* and whale meat was already cooked. As it was cooling, Masu and the chief's wife made Eskimo ice cream. Qunigrak and his cousin rested, for it had been hard work hauling the whale meat from the dugout where it had been buried the week before.

While they were eating, the chief told of the fun he had had as he was gathering the snared ducks. Curious, Amak asked him, "How many ducks did we catch?" He challenged her to go to the boat and count them, for he knew Amak was capable of counting. Malquay stayed near the boat and listened while her sister counted the ducks aloud.

"*Atausiq* [one], *malluk* [two], *pinasut* [three], *sisamat* [four]…" and on up to the number of thirty-one ducks.

When she came back, she said to them, "I"ll pluck ducks while we are sailing," and Malquay echoed, 'Me too, eh Grandma?" Her grandmother nodded, smiling at her dear little Malquay.

They sat down to eat their supper, and when they had finished, Qunigrak said, 'It is time for us to sail, and late tonight we will be home."

It was a beautiful evening with just enough wind to carry them on their way, and the two *umiaks* sailed together. As usual, the girls went to sleep the minute they went to bed in the boat.

Qunigrak sang a song which his mother interpreted as a song of his anticipation of returning home to see his second family. He had missed them and now wondered how his little baby daughter and his wife had spent a week while he was away. He thought, "They'll be glad to see me home and to receive fresh *muktuk* and game birds."

They traveled somewhat slower than before as the tide was against them. But they arrived not long after sunset. When they came near the mouth of Unalakleet River, Qunigrak took down the sail and poled the *umiak* up the stream as far as possible. Then, with his mother steering, he hauled the boat with a rope the rest of the way to their own pier at the mouth of a slough.

# III

# CHALAVALUK

# 9
# CHALAVALUK

My FATHER's grandmother, Chalavuluk, lived in the river village of Pastolik on the bank of a tributary of the Yukon River near St. Michael. She lived with her parents, Mr. and Mrs. Yukuniaqag. She and her people were Yup'ik Eskimos, who inhabited the northernmost part of a vast low region near the mouth of the Yukon River close to the Bering Sea. Her old village now has been long deserted by its people. These Eskimos are distinctly different from the Northern Unalik and Iñupiaq Eskimos. Their language is different and in the early days they could not communicate easily with the northern Eskimo so the Yup'ik and Iñupiaq rarely associated with each other. But after the Russians and then the Americans settled in Alaska, these Eskimos began to travel more widely.

The northern Eskimos were sometimes called Malemutes, a term which was first used by the Unalik Eskimos to designate the Iñupiaq Eskimos of Unalakleet when they first emigrated southward from the arctic regions. No one in either the Yukon Region or Unalakleet remembers how long ago they moved to their present home.

Their physical features are quite different from the northern tribes too. Their skin is fair and most individuals are short and usually small boned. Differences in diet might have been one of the factors that affected their coloring. The northern Eskimos relied largely on sea mammals and caribou for their subsistence, while the Yup'ik thrive on freshwater fish, game birds, seal, and fur-bearing land mammals.

My great-grandmother, according to the reports of the older Yupiks, had fine features and light skin, and was a beautiful woman. She was the only girl in the family. Her parents loved her dearly, although in our traditional culture, male offspring—not females—were considered a blessing to a couple. Like a male child, she was taught to hunt, and she received manual training. Her father trained her in the many skills of hunting until she was old enough to marry.

When her parents talked to her about her future place as a wife and offered to train her for that role, she let them know that she would prefer to help them in their old age rather than support a husband. Also, she did not wish to be married at an early age. But when she was thirteen her mother tried very hard to encourage her to learn how to sew and do the other skills expected of a woman who would eventually become a housewife. To her mother's consternation and disappointment, Chalavaluk consistently refused to accept offers of marriage from the young men of the village. She was one young girl who dared to defy the traditions of her race. She was not afraid of ridicule, nor punishment by the leaders of the village for her intransigence. She would do what she thought was best for herself.

Then one day when she was out checking her snares for ducks, she met an older man who had come to her village from St. Michael for a visit. As she was expertly paddling her kayak she passed him by quickly, and to her surprise he didn't seem to notice her skill or her beauty. All afternoon she felt indignant about this man who had failed to notice her womanly charm. But later her attitude changed and the episode caused her to respect him the more for his lack of interest in her. She began to contemplate another meeting with him. After she had retrieved the ducks she had caught and reset the tangled snares, she decided to return home quickly to try to satisfy her curiosity about this unknown man.

When she arrived home, her father, as usual, appeared on the beach and offered to help her place the kayak in its berth. After this chore was done her father carried the ducks to their igloo. She and her mother plucked the feathers immediately so they could have fresh duck for supper. While they were doing this, the man she had seen that afternoon entered the igloo. Chalavaluk's father welcomed him and invited him to eat supper with them. The girl felt uncomfortable in the presence of this older man. He apparently had known her father, having met him several times at St. Michael, for during the supper and later they talked of many things. He appeared to feel at home with them during his visit at their village. And when they had Eskimo dances she saw that he was a good, lively dancer.

He stayed at the village for a long time and her parents seemed to like him. To her surprise he didn't propose to her. Thereafter she learned to accept him as a companion only. She did not fall in love with him, but she appreciated his skill at hunting the sea mammals which were necessary for survival, especially then, at the beginning of the winter season. Later in the winter he returned home to his parents, but he left with a promise that he would be back the following year.

Chalavaluk missed him. Many times thereafter, she pictured herself with him for life. She began to realize that she needed someone to give her protection and security. Her parents also missed his amiable personality, but she tried not to show her anxiety about his return to the village. And if he should propose, she wondered, should she accept his offer?

Fall came again and one stormy day, late in the evening, he came unexpectedly into their igloo. He was covered with hoarfrost from head to foot and he appeared exhausted. The storm, he said later, had made his trip a hazardous ordeal. But, he reported to them with pride, his lead dog had successfully found the trail which led to their village. His dogs had gone straight for the nearest igloo. "When I entered your tunnel, I did not know it was your igloo."

Chalavaluk's father replied, "You're welcome to stay with us this night. It is too stormy to move about tonight." And he urged his wife to lay out food for him on the grass mat.

That night was the beginning of a union of a new family within an old family. As time passed, Chalavaluk's parents were not surprised when the evidence of close companionship made itself known. Chalavaluk found herself sewing for her future husband.

Toward spring, perhaps, there would be a wedding feast. To many, especially her family's friends, it was expected, but not to the old skeptics.

After their marriage, Chalavaluk and her husband-companion did many things together. Her parents were pleased about their daughter's success in marriage, and their son-in-law appeared to be contented and happy.

During their first summer together her husband decided to build a separate igloo near her parents' home. This plan did not please Chalavaluk, for she loved her parents. She did not consent to his plan until he promised her that they would share their food with her mother and father, and that they would be able to join them at mealtimes. He explained his reason for the move. Since they were expecting a baby to be born soon, he did not wish her parents to be disturbed at night when their baby cried. She then appreciated his thoughtfulness in being so concerned over her parents' comfort.

They gathered driftwood and dug blocks of sod to construct their new home. Chalavaluk and her mother collected grass for insulating the interior of the igloo, and the girl learned how to weave beautiful grass mats for the walls and floor. She also made the seal-gut window and other furnishings. With the help of her father, the new igloo was built before the first cold spell of the fall.

Soon after they moved in, her husband asked her if she would like to take a trip to St. Michael to meet his parents. She approved of his idea, and after much preparation they left by dog team. Both settled comfortably in a sitting position, taking turns driving the team. Chalavaluk knew her parents were happy to have their daughter go away on a well-deserved trip. This was to be a short visit before freezeup, her husband told her parents, and they should not worry, for the travelers would return in a few days.

And it was not very long before they came back to their home, bringing with them beautiful Eskimo parkas, traditional gifts from his parents. The parkas were made of rock squirrels, trimmed with the very best wolf and wolverine fur.

# 10
# INFANTICIDE

THERE WERE many forces and traditions that shaped the lives of the Eskimos, and Chalavaluk knew them well. One of the most pervading, and often heart rending, traditions was the way they looked upon the birth of male and female children.

If an Eskimo wife bore a male child in those days, her husband considered himself a fortunate man. Their lineage would be preserved through their son, they would be blessed with a future hunter to take the father's place, the son would provide food for the unfortunate people of his village, and the son's arrival would assure the father's status as a well respected man.

A man who becomes a great hunter in the course of his life is a hero to his people. The woman's status was always subordinate. She could bring happiness to her husband and family by bearing his children and by being a good worker. If she could not carry out her expected duties at home, such as the butchering and preserving of her hunter husband's catch, then he would hire a second wife to help her. It was an honor to have a husband who was a great hunter and had more than one wife, but the second wife had even less status and was taken into the family only as a helper to the first wife.

The birth of a daughter did not necessarily bring happiness to a young couple. It depended largely on the village elders and husbands. The decision to keep the child or to destroy her would be made by the chief and village council. The prospects for a second female child in consecutive years were rarely good.

It was the mother herself who was expected to carry out the dreaded task of destroying her girl baby when the occasion arose. She had no voice in the matter. She knew the custom was established to make allowance for the economic conditions in the community at any given time. It was a pathetic experience for the women, a pitiful and inhuman act. Sometimes women left their homes, but the majority did not have any alternative. They were faced with an inescapable situation that had to be accepted.

Chalavaluk would soon give birth to a baby. She was thankful that her mother had taught her the signs of labor. Now Chalavaluk and her mother listened as the Eskimo midwife gave the pregnant girl her first lessons in what to expect and what to do when the labor pains started. She encouraged the mother-to-be to continue to do the usual household duties and not to sleep too late in the morning. She explained clearly that she must wish for a male child. She must get up early and go outdoors to the horizon, and the woman taught her how to interpret the signs of good and evil weather. She should also watch for any unusual animal activity nearby. Then, after she had done this each morning, she could go into the igloo and do her chores for her husband's welfare. The custom she most dreaded was that allowing the midwife to drop hairless, live baby porcupines onto her chest and abdomen one by one. The object of this ritual was to encourage the young woman to start hoping for a male child.

Chalavaluk cried when she entered the igloo. She would have to endure all these practices of her race, even to bearing her child out in a little shack called the *caluxverak*. When her time came, she would stay there until she was considered purified, when the baby's umbilical cord was healed. Midwives or their own mothers took care of new mothers. If a woman gave birth during the winter or while she was traveling, her husband would build a temporary snowhouse for her. She would live in the snow igloo until she was strong enough to travel on. Her husband would help her to cover the floor with thick woven willow mats on which would be laid dry hay for a mattress.

Chalavaluk considered herself blessed when the baby came early one spring morning. But to her disappointment, her child was a girl. To her it did not matter whether she bore a baby boy or girl, but she knew that to her husband and family her baby girl would be unwelcome.

She heard her mother announce the birth of the baby girl in a whisper, "*Agnak* [a female], Chalavaluk!" Both women trembled as they recalled what the chief of Pastolik had said: "All female infants shall be killed this year. There is not enough food for the existing people here."

This order was given to the childbearing women, Chalavaluk among them. She knew there was no way she could alter this economic and moral law. Furthermore, Chalavaluk had no power, nor had anyone else, not even the chief's wife or daughter, to defer the decision. Chalavaluk covered her face and grieved.

"How can I bear this destruction of my own flesh and blood?" She hugged her baby girl and vowed, "I have you, my little *banuning* [daughter], at least while you're within my reach. I will always love you."

At this moment she felt more secure having her mother near her. She talked to the baby as the helpless infant was feeding at her breast. Chalavaluk tried very hard to subdue her emotion, until her mother, grieving too, spoke to her about the baby, which they had named Chikuk.

Her mother explained that the women are always subject to the mores and taboos of the community, even in their private lives, "Because we must help our husbands to provide us with a livelihood for our family. Perhaps your next baby will be a boy. But in the meantime, give much love to your little Chikuk while you are in isolation. The feeling of loss will be erased as the time passes. I will take care of you until the baby's umbilical is healed. Your father will give Chikuk a traditional name."

After her mother had left, Chalavaluk nursed her baby and watched the doomed infant. Each time she nursed the baby she would hug Chikuk closely.

Many sleepless nights Chalavaluk spent alone. Perhaps she deplored and inwardly rebelled against the customs of her community. Or, perhaps, she regretted being born a woman. No one but herself could change the unpleasant situation she would soon have to face. Her love for her first-born child was so great that now nothing else mattered. In the early hours of morning she left the scene of the most agonizing experience of her life.

It was quickly heard throughout the village that Chalavaluk had disappeared, leaving her child in the tunnel entrance of her parents' igloo. The search for Chalavaluk began immediately and continued all that summer. Only one clue was found: Someone had seen footprints on the beach, but the high tide erased them before a real lead could be established.

The young mother's brave action greatly affected the members of the village council. They decided to save Chikuk's life in exchange for the loss of her mother. The baby would be raised by her grandparents. The consequences were even more far-reaching, for Chalavaluk's self-sacrifice in instinctively seeking a way to save her baby signaled the end of the custom of infanticide in the village. But, sadly, the instigator of this sweeping change had to suffer permanent separation from her loved ones to finally impress upon the chief and council that such deaths would not end famines.

# 11
# CHALAVALUK'S ADVENTURE

CHALAVALUK WAS trained to walk fast at night and now she was very glad of it. She walked until she came to her pack, which she had prepared and hidden in anticipation of her departure. She stopped for a moment to put her pack over her shoulders and settle it in place, and then continued her trek, following the beach. She did not ease her pace until she was beyond St. Michael. Continuing on, she arrived at Pitmiktalik and was relieved when she found the village people still sleeping. She decided that when the early tide covered the seashore's edge she would sleep among the driftwood.

Before she came to a good resting place, she stopped long enough to eat and drink some cool water. The tide began to overtake her, so about noon she found a nook under a big driftwood tree stump. She covered the sides with more driftwood, then gathered dry grass and laid it on the floor in her enclosure. She slept here before resuming her flight to Unalakleet, which she had decided would be her goal.

She traveled by dark and took three nights to reach Unalakleet village. None of the villagers were awake and she hid herself in a sailing *umiak*, under its cargo of neatly packed sealskins which were securely tied to either side of the wooden frame. She soon fell asleep.

When Chalavaluk awoke, she could feel the rolling of the boat. She wondered how far they would travel, but to her it did not really matter. Her only concern was to remain securely hidden and not be found for several days. With thoughts of her baby, tears came, but the tears helped to ease her pain. When she heard the Eskimos in the *umiak* speak she could not understand them; their language seemed strange and abrupt to Chalavaluk. She grew cramped, thirsty, hungry, and hoped they would reach their destination soon. But she was very determined.

The next day the strange Eskimos landed the boat and all went ashore. This gave Chalavaluk an opportunity to crawl out of hiding, stretch herself, eat some of her food and drink some water. Then she hid herself once more. She wondered if these people were sailing back to their own village. Chalavaluk was happy that these unknown Eskimos had not discovered her in her hiding place. She heard them coming back to the boat and they sailed again. The rolling of the sea put her to sleep once more. She realized she must have slept for several hours because when she awoke and peeked through the openings between the skins, she noticed the sun was lower. What a relief not to have been found and molested or even thrown overboard.

The following day, the Eskimos landed again, at the village of Teller. After they went ashore, she watched for a chance to leave the boat herself, to exercise, eat, and do her chores. This time the men stayed overnight at the village, so when she went back to her hiding place she had a chance to fix her nook so that it would be more comfortable. She slept soundly, and then she woke up suddenly as the men began piling more things over her. These Eskimo traders had evidently bought more Native supplies from the people of the village. Not long after they sailed the weight of the material became unbearable so Chalavaluk decided she had better expose herself to escape from being crushed by the pressure.

When Chalavaluk crawled out of her hiding place, there was great excitement among the crew. They all talked at once and shouted to each other and looked at her in a most hideous way. Finally, their captain came over and talked to her, but she did not understand a word of what he was saying. Chalavaluk was afraid, so she collapsed and cried loudly. Some of the men touched her on her shoulder as a friendly gesture and offered water and food. As she wiped her tears she managed to nod her head to let them know that she appreciated their offer. Oh, what a blessing to live and not to have been molested or thrown overboard. They evidently decided to take her all the way to Wales, which was their village. Although she was hungry she did not eat the food. Instead, she sat and watched the new scenery as the *umiak* sailed near the edge of the seashore.

During the rest of the trip, one of the strangers tried to talk to her by making signs with his hands when it was time to drink and eat. His smile made Chalavaluk feel more comfortable and gave her some assurance that they would remain friendly. Chalavaluk sat up straight on a bundle of fur. Her whole body ached from remaining crouched and frigid for days, hiding in the boat. She heard a seagull calling to its companion, at first from a far distance. The call sounded familiar and helped to lessen her fear. Curious, she scanned the sky to get a glimpse of it. She looked at the sea and traced the receding waves as they softly rolled away toward the mainland, their action resembling her longing to reach the beach.

"*Quyahnaa* [thanks], we're finally approaching the land," she thought.

Her pulse beat faster and she felt warmer and happier, with a brighter hope for the future. She watched the seagull flying overhead as if to guide the *umiak* to its destination.

She reached into her hiding place, grasped her mittens, put them on, and brushed the fur. The old familiar mittens were a comfort at this moment of crisis in her life. Now the sea became glossy and in her imagination it mirrored a picture of her home, the river, their *umiak* and the gulls screeching over the remnants of the fish which her mother used to throw to them. She followed the birds' flight hoping they would not disappear from her sight. For how long she sat thinking about home she did not know. Then her recollection was displaced by the sight of a cliff above the sea as they were passing by.

They continued sailing along the high and irregular promontory of the cliff which now paralleled the shore. She could hear the breakers' rhythmic boom! boom! and see the spray as the sea rushed over the table of sand onto the beach.

Shortly after sunset the dark shadows of the mountain spread over the tundra and the coastline. This change of light affected Chalavaluk again, and her anxiety about her destination made her tense.

Then she heard the steersman yelling to the others and simultaneously pointing to the land with a smile on his face. They began to chatter, but she could not understand what the excitement was all about until one man came over and made gestures for her to stand up. She got up and looked where he was pointing ahead. There above several igloo mounds, gray smoke was rising and disappearing into the sky. Since they were yet well off and sailing beneath the level of the beach, the size of the village was hard to determine. People were gathered on the beach to welcome the seafarers. They all appeared to be excited over the return of their relatives.

As she sat down again, she was thankful that her wish for an end to the voyage had come true. Now she wanted to rest from the fatigue and strain of the night. But she began to wonder once more about her safety. How would the village receive her? She held onto her amulet and asked it to help her face these strangers and induce them to offer her their home to live in. Perhaps she might become a slave, or even a second wife to a great hunter. She earnestly vowed that as long as she was treated kindly she willingly would accept whatever role was assigned to her in her new environment.

Soon they landed and the captain of the *umiak* gestured to her to get off the boat. He led her to a woman who shook hands with her pleasantly.

"Take her to our igloo; she will live with us," he commanded, and now Chalavaluk understood.

The woman took her arm gently and smiled at her and led her toward the path.

"*Kaq'qeen* [come]."

Chalavaluk understood the word, an invitation to join her. She walked lightly with this new friend through the village and its collection of small and large igloos. The woman led her to the entrance of a large igloo which was located in the middle of the community near an even larger council house. Now she learned that the captain of the *umiak* was the chief of the village.

## 12
## CHALAVALUK BEGINS A NEW LIFE

CHALAVALUK FOLLOWED her hostess very carefully as they passed through the igloo's tunnel entrance. They lowered themselves on a crude ladder which extended into a spacious and well stocked storeroom. Since the storeroom was only partly lighted by a seal-oil lamp they could not see clearly at first, so they stood still. Chalavaluk noticed many types of preserved foods, and felt overwhelmed as she identified the contents of the seal pokes. Most were filled with dried *ugruk* and fish and were neatly stacked side by side on raised wooden shelves. One shelf contained pokes filled with rendered oil, greens, berries, roots, preserved eggs, and ducks and geese that had been smothered in their own fat. Other seal-poke containers were packed to their capacity with cooked two- by four-inch slices of *muktuk*. Adjacent to the seal pokes were *ugruk* stomach containers filled with a mixture of tomcod liver paste and blackberries. There were also wooden containers filled with different kinds of berries.

Chalavaluk's mouth watered as she thought of her favorite dish, a mixture of cranberry sauce and blackberries. One other dish she noticed was *achaagluk*. To prepare this Eskimo dessert, sweet beachgrass is wilted, cooled, and chopped, then laid outdoors in a wooden container to ferment in the warmth of the summer sun. In the fall when the wild strawberries are ripe, they are gathered and mixed into the fermented beachgrass. The resulting concoction is particularly relished by the Eskimos. Other wild edible greens, such as two kinds of rhubarb prepared like the sweet beachgrass, were also preserved in the storeroom.

Seeing such nutritious food and realizing that the people were treating her kindly, Chalavaluk became optimistic. She recalled the seasonal hunting at her former home. There was much gathering of ripe berries and wild greens, and the familiar sights at the new place aroused her hopes that she might gather such food for her new family, the chief's. The mere thought of being able to go out into the wilderness alone to do her share of the food gathering for these kind people gave her a satisfying feeling and she looked forward to offering her services.

At this moment Wiyana, the chief's wife, took her hand and led her through a dark passageway into another room, the Eskimo kitchen. It was quite large and comfortable since it was not cluttered with many unnecessary items. In the center of the kitchen, suspended over the coals of the fire, was a clay pot filled with food being cooked for their next meal. By the opposite wall was a crude wooden table which also could serve as a cutting board. Shelves on the other end of the wall were stacked with several sizes of wooden bowls and platters. The Eskimo woman's *ulus* [knives] were also visible, neatly placed in holders on the wall. All these underground rooms were lighted with large and small seal-oil lamps, provided with braided lake-moss wicks. Light from a single window in the roof somewhat eased the darkness. The food cooking, with its familiar, palatable scent, made Chalavaluk hungry.

They left the kitchen and walked through another passageway until they came to the foot of a ladder which was raised to the entrance to another room above their heads. She climbed up at the heels of her hostess who opened the trap door. They entered a brightly lit, spacious room. On a long platform set against one wall lay furs which Chalavaluk recognized as bedding. On the left side she discerned what she thought was her hostess's bed, and on the other side was laid the chief's and his younger son's bed. She wondered if they would provide her with a bedroom or just a bed. The fireplace was directly below a window cut in the roof. The primitive Eskimos called this *kilak'lugok*, meaning an entrance for a good spirit who might pay a visit to their home at any time. The window opening also served the home as a vent and a skylight.

Chalavaluk was given a straw mat to sit on, and was asked to take off her mukluks and her clothing. Her hostess did likewise, since once inside it was customary to replace outdoor clothing with indoor clothes. Wiyana gave her a squirrel-skin housecoat and caribou slippers to wear. She also was given squirrel-skin slacks which were worn with the fur inside.

Using sign language, Chalavaluk indicated to her hostess that she would like to bathe. She was taken to a steambath room which was built adjacent to the chief's living room. There she found a bowl of water, a grass-root sponge, and hand-rubbed soft grass for a towel. After her bath she was ready for her meal.

But at this moment the chief entered with his two sons and another woman who was carrying a baby on her back. Chalavaluk partially understood now. She felt more cheerful and smiled as she shook hands with the newcomers.

The chief said, "My sons and I will eat in the *kargii*; I know our guest is hungry. She hasn't eaten for a long time, Wiyana, so don't feed her too much food this evening, just a couple of bowls of broth and a small helping of *atchagluk*."

"There will be a welcome dance for the travelers and our guest tonight," continued the chief. "Chalavaluk, you come and join us. We will not expect any strenuous dancing, but the next time we celebrate in the fall festival you will be permitted to do your own interpretative dancing."

"*Aaoag* [yes]!"

'My *newborik* [second wife] will provide you with your material needs," he added.

The chief and his sons went out to the *kargii*.

After supper the chief's wives, Wiyana and Kunookcheen, changed their clothing for beautifully made fur parkas. Chalavaluk was given Wiyana's parka and mittens, but she expressed a desire to wear her own garb. She was given permission to do so.

At the welcome celebration the chief explained to the people how Chalavaluk had come to Wales with them.

"Under unknown circumstances and through her own will, Chalavaluk decided to leave her own home in Pastolik and stow away on our boat, not knowing where we would bring her."

He requested that the people welcome her as their guest and further explained that she had accepted the offer to live with his family.

"And to show your kindness and as a gesture of acceptance, we will dance in her honor."

Chalavaluk joined them in the dance, and her own quiet, graceful movements portrayed her appreciation, especially to the chief and his family.

She was permitted to leave the dance shortly after meeting some servants and all the notables, including the chief's hunters. Before she reached the door, however, she felt an arm lift, by a new admirer, perhaps. It was the chief's younger son, whose name she recalled as Aquwealuk. He held her arm all the way to their igloo. He couldn't pronounce her name very well yet.

"You must be very tired, Chalacktoon. I hope you will have a good night's rest and sleep." He opened the tunnel door and held it for her until she reached the passageway.

# IV

# CHIKUK

# 13
# CHIKUK'S WISH

MANY OF the old Eskimo villages of the Lower Yukon River Delta are now ghost sites. Pastolik is one of these. Most likely the citizens moved to neighboring villages to seek employment. When the Russian-American Company established its trading post at St. Michael, the Eskimo people from the small surrounding communities had a market at which to trade their furs and dried fish in return for staple goods, clothing, tools, or guns.

Fur-bearing animals were so plentiful during those early days that every able person went trapping during the winter. The Russians extended credit to the Natives to enable them to buy traps and other necessary goods, then accepted their catch to pay off their debts. The company then sent the furs to Russia where there was a ready market. The Natives stored the salmon in their caches as soon as the fish were dry enough. They were tied together in bundles of fifty. In the fall, when overland travel by dog team became possible, the company bought the dried fish, which was not only fed to the dogs, but also eaten by the people.

Pastolik Natives were in a good position to sell their fish and furs to the Russian traders, for theirs was the closest village to St. Michael. The Pastolik River is situated just a few miles east of the delta of the Yukon River and empties into Norton

Sound. The distance from the village to St. Michael was about thirty or forty miles. The Eskimos of Pastolik usually traveled by boat to St. Michael during the fall months to sell their fish. Now that Alaska had been purchased by the United States, the Alaska Commercial Company had replaced the old Russian-American Company. The town, though, was still predominantly owned by Russians.

Chikuk, Chalavaluk's daughter, was raised by her grandparents at Pastolik. When she found out that they were not her real parents, her curiosity was aroused and she felt unhappy, especially when she heard about the predicament which caused her mother to leave her home and baby. Now that she was a teenage girl, she would frequently ponder her mother's disappearance.

When she was playing outdoors alone, she would often climb the nearest mound to stare at the landscape to the north. There, she would imagine her mother walking away towards that large sea. Chikuk would scan the horizon with teary eyes, suppressing an urgent need to unravel the mystery by retracing her mother's path. This emotional restlessness made her yearn for just a glimpse of her mother. And when she daydreamed, she would pretend that she was a heroine, and would rescue her mother.

"Maybe I will travel like my mother and find happiness somewhere beyond the sea," she thought. Daydreaming about a reunion with her mother made her feel better.

One day her grandfather, Yukuniagag, revealed to his family his plans to move to St. Michael. He explained to his family that there might be a better chance of selling some of his catch of fish and furs to the *Copaniskaks*, the white men's company. Furthermore, he expressed his desire to work for the company, perhaps as a laborer or a longshoreman.

# 14
# CHIKUK'S ENGAGEMENT AND WEDDING

Yukuniagag had to get up early one morning, since he had been chilled during the night. He built a fire in the stove to warm the tent in which they had been living temporarily since they arrived in St. Michael. As he sat with his parka on, he planned his daily activity. "I will have to search for a house to live in today. The month of October is already upon us and soon the lakes and rivers will be frozen over. This means I will have to work or make a living by hunting. If I can find a house today, we'll move in by evening."

After breakfast he reviewed his plans with his wife. "I will ask my friend, Moses, right away. Perhaps he can come with me to town today. He knows the Cossacks and other people of St. Michael."

Yukuniagag left to find his friend.

Moses was glad to help Yukuniagag in his search for a house. He suggested that they interview first a Russian, Sergei Ivanoff, whose companions had left for Siberia in a Russian steamship. They found Ivanoff's home, and Moses knocked on the door before they entered. Yukuniagag was glad that he had asked Moses to go with him, otherwise he might have gone into the house without knocking, as was the Eskimo custom. The Cossack opened the door and invited them to enter. Moses introduced his friend to Mr. Ivanoff. They sat down at the table for hot coffee and, speaking in Russian, Moses described his friend's housing problem. He would pay for the house by working and trapping furs.

After a lengthy conversation, Moses turned to Yukuniagag to interpret, "Mr. Ivanoff said that there is a house that you can either rent or buy and pay for within a year's time. It has two bedrooms, but it is not very big. It would not be very expensive and perhaps your wife might be able to sew Eskimo clothing and sell it to help pay expenses."

After he inspected the house, Yukuniagag decided to buy it. Moses then explained that every month on the same day he must pay twenty-five dollars. Mr. Ivanoff had the bill of sale ready for him before the men left. Since Yukuniagag had saved enough money, he made the first payment.

So Yukuniagag and his family moved into the white man's house. The structure had no modern facilities, but the family enjoyed living in a completely furnished house, an igloo built on the surface of the ground, with windows on the side walls, and with a stove which had to be fed all day in order to keep the house warm. Moreover they would sleep on a bed raised on four legs with springs and a mattress. Every new experience was exciting to each of them. The complete change from their old habit of living involved much more activity, with many different housekeeping chores to be performed.

Mr. Ivanoff became their mentor. From him Chikuk learned how to keep house. She also attended school, but not being used to spending hours in a classroom, when she came home she acted like an animal, which after being leashed, was set free to do whatever it wished. She learned to speak in three languages: St. Michael Eskimo dialect, English, and Russian. Yukuniagag's family learned more and more with the help of Sergei Ivanoff's advice, especially how to cope with strange food, clothing, and many other confusing aspects of life in the white man's town.

Now that Yukuniagag had to become a wage earner, Sergei

hired him as his employee. Sergei was in charge of the Alaska Commercial restaurant, and he needed a dishwasher and handyman. Yukuniagag was very helpful to Sergei. Although his wife was left alone at home, she was kept very busy sewing. Her granddaughter and husband did not return home until late afternoon. Yukuniagag brought coal and leftover food from the restaurant. During the weekends Chikuk, too, worked for Sergei and her grandmother kept her company. Chikuk received valuable training and she was now quite a capable young woman. Within a year's time she had learned how to dress properly and how to act in white society. She understood her role as a lady.

By spring the whole family had adjusted to this new life. And this led to another exciting event for Chikuk. She fell in love. She and her parents usually had their meals at Sergei's home and she would help to prepare the meals. In the evening she would study the Russian language with Mr. Ivanoff. This companionship was a pleasant interlude for both parties. Before very long, Sergei began to court Chikuk seriously. Since he was now of age himself, he found that he needed a wife, and Chikuk needed someone to protect her. He invited the whole family to attend the Russian Orthodox Church with him and soon they were accepted as members. When the official information on the family history was entered into the church records, including the disappearance of Chikuk's mother, Sergei's sympathy for Chikuk hastened his decision to propose to her. He asked her grandparents first, and they gave their consent to their granddaughter's future husband. He then gave Chikuk a ring as a sign of his deep love for her. However, it took her a long time to realize what it meant to be betrothed to a white man. He was very patient with her.

They made plans for their wedding with the Russian priest, who explained the marriage rites to them. The date was set for the month of June, before the arrival of the annual ship from the States.

Instead of a simple Eskimo marriage ceremony, Chikuk had an elaborate wedding according to the ritual of the Russian Orthodox Church.

The marriage of Sergei and Chikuk was one of the earliest, if not the first, formal intermarriages at St. Michael. Sergei's request to marry Chikuk might not have been accepted if Chikuk's family had not been members of the Russian Orthodox faith. The same priest who had performed their baptism also conducted the marriage ceremony in the new Russian church at St. Michael.

What a colorful marriage rite for Chikuk to participate in. Compared to the traditional Eskimo ceremony, it was quite overwhelming. The bridegroom and the bride were given tall candles, taken in front of the lectern and instructed to kneel. Sergei knelt to the left of his bride. Two crown bearers stood behind the couple and held crowns at arm's length over their heads for an hour while the priest performed the marriage ceremony. Sergei prompted Chikuk when to make her responses so she would not be embarrassed. The priest lit two candles, turned and faced the bridal pair and swung his censer slowly around them. Sergei glanced at his bride who appeared to be quite placidly toying with her bouquet of wild tundra flowers. She smiled quickly at him. He loved her dearly. He wished that his mother, who lived in Russia, could have attended his wedding. He would write her a letter about his little bride and tell her why he married an Eskimo girl. A tall head deacon wearing an alb of silver cloth stood opposite the priest and read the vows to them, his words intermingled with the music from the unseen choir loft. When the deacon finished reading the litany the priest turned to the bridal pair and, in a sing-song voice, he concluded the main part of the ceremony.

"Amen!" The unseen choir sang the affirmation.

Then the couple exchanged rings and were blessed by the priest. The Epistle was read to them while the choir sang psalms. The bridal pair stood up, the candles were taken from them and the couple and the crown bearers marched around the lectern three times. They then stood before the audience as the priest proclaimed them to be Mr. and Mrs. Sergei Ivanoff. Finally, arm in arm, Chikuk and Sergei went outdoors and received the congratulations of the church members.

The reception was given at the home of Chikuk's great-aunt and great-uncle, Ahlugga and Iglukuk Kameroff.

# 15

# YUKUNIAGAG AND AHLUGGA HUNT SEA MAMMALS

Two-year-old Stephan missed his great-grandfather, Yukuniagag, who had left on a seal-hunting trip with his brother-in-law, Ahlugga. Every day Chikuk took her son out for walks to amuse him during Yukuniagag's absence. When the old man returned with two *ugruks* and three ringed seals, Stevie followed him everywhere as he unloaded his sled. Yukuniagag allowed the tot to carry his personal things into their tent. Several times before Stevie reached the entrance, he tumbled down, but he made no whimper. He picked himself up and resumed his task, babbling to the nearest person and smiling broadly. Chikuk watched the excited little boy who tried so hard to talk to his great-grandpa whose expressions were a bit too guttural at times for the youngster to understand.

Chikuk was not strong enough to lift the heavy pieces of ugruk meat and blubber. "Sergei will soon be home for supper, Grandpa. He can help you lift the heaviest pieces onto the wheel-barrow," Chikuk suggested. He agreed, and he and his companion followed Chikuk to the tent where she presented them with hot tea and Eskimo doughnuts. While they were having this welcome tea break, Sergei came in with a smile.

"Yuku, and Uncle Ahlugga, you are lucky hunters," Sergei said. "I'm sure Steve and Chikuk are just as thankful as I am for the fresh meat you brought home." He sat down by his little family as his wife poured him some tea also.

"Sergei, Grandpa and Uncle need help. Some parts of the *ugruk* are heavy. You'll have to help them carry the pieces to the cache." They all went out again, and Chikuk took a pot and *ulu* with her to prepare some of the fresh meat for supper. Sergei spoke to Stevie in Russian and Yukuniagag talked to the boy in the Yup'ik Eskimo dialect.

The family decided to preserve the meat, blubber, and skins during the following week. Ahlugga and Yukuniagag set the *ugruk* on a wooden platform for Chikuk and Iglukuk, Mrs. Yukuniagag's sister, to work on. Iglukuk denuded the sealskins to make them into seal pokes; Chikuk stripped the ugruk meat for drying. The Eskimo men then hung the meat on the racks, while Sergei took care of Stevie and kept the fire going. Several days were spent on the project.

To dry the *ugruk* skins, the men made eight-foot by twelve-foot oblong frames. They cut loops about six inches apart around the circumference of each skin and then the two men threaded the slits with babiche, beginning from the head, and alternately wound the rope onto the frame. When the hide dried, it would be used for boot soles.

One young *ugruk* skin, with its flippers, was prepared by Yukuniagag for the process of molting. A thin layer of blubber which had been left intact on the inner part of the skin would cause the hair to molt in time. The skin was folded in half, then quarters and tied securely with a rope. Then it was placed in a wooden container, to be left for two weeks.

*Ugruk* is a prized food of the Eskimos and may be prepared in a number of ways. One of the celebrated feasts is what the Eskimos call *Igunak*. *Ugruk* skin is stretched onto a frame and laid on a platform with a forty-five degree angle. Excess blubber is taken off and cleaned masu roots are placed on this skin plate, along with dried *ugruk* meat and cooked flippers. From this the diners eat, dipping the food in cured *ugruk* oil by scraping it with their *ulus*. For dessert they usually would have berries and *Ahyu* tea. This meal could be compared in white man's terms perhaps most closely with a combination of steak and Limburger cheese.

Yukuniagag and Ahlugga scraped the inner skin of the *ugruk* thoroughly before they hung it up to dry. When cured, this skin is usually used to make soles for fancy mukluks, for children's boots and slippers. It is used also as a kayak covering and for making babiche.

Meanwhile, Chikuk watched her great-aunt Iglukuk scrape off the outer muscles of the intestines, which would be saved for food, then she placed the intestines in a saltwater solution for four hours. After a rinsing in fresh water, they were inflated with care and stretched out to dry. When dry, the intestinal tubing was cut, flattened and rolled into five-inch widths. The plastic-like skin was then stored away in a seal-poke container where eventually it would be made into a raincoat or cover throw. It was also often used as a soft container for baby food, to hold seal oil and to make bandages. Chikuk learned a great deal by watching Iglukuk and listening to her directions.

Her great-aunt also showed her how to scrape the muscles off the *ugruk* stomach. First, the stomach was inflated with air; second, the balloon's outer layer of meat was scraped off, and the scrapings were saved for food. The outer layer of muscles of the intestines were similarly prepared.

The stomach is primarily used as a container for a mixture of tomcod oil and cooked liver-berry, a dessert dish, as well as for greens and other prepared foods.

The last chore the women had to do was to store the dried meat, which was preserved by the rendered seal oil and placed in seal pokes. The seal blubber was also stripped and dropped into a poke. All this food would be kept in a cellar during the winter.

Chikuk asked her great-aunt Iglukuk to live with her family in their house at St. Michael. "You can keep us company and we'll share our food with you and my uncle." Her suggestion was a hint that Chikuk's health was failing. She knew her aunt could prepare Eskimo dishes in an orderly and appetizing way for the family.

The day they finished their work, she asked Iglukuk to make Eskimo ice cream while she baked fresh bread. The work during the past week had been a wonderful get-together, a cooperative experience that Chikuk had enjoyed tremendously. It was like the life she had had when she was a child at Pastolik, she recalled.

"Auntie, I'm sure if grandmother were still living she would appreciate your kindnesses and the help you've given to Sergei and me. If anything unforeseen should happen to us, Auntie," Chikuk said cryptically, "feel free to help yourself to the *ugruk* meat and oil we've preserved this past week."

"Grandpa," she continued, turning to Yukuniagag, "we can take some of the *ugruk* meat and oil to Egg Island. You and my uncle Ahlugga can pick murre eggs from the cliff and Iglukuk and I will pick duck eggs and cranberries. Sergei, when would we be able to leave?"

"Soon, I hope," he answered.

The following week Sergei and Yukuniagag were very busy putting away a fresh supply of groceries and merchandise. Sergei did not tell his wife, but he was not sure he could find an eligible cook to take his place for the duration of the trip. Yet, he did not want to disappoint her. Luckily a substitute was found and readied to take over in the morning. When Sergei went home that evening, he gave orders to the family to do the packing.

He smiled at his wife. She appeared to be happy. He hoped her appetite would improve, he thought to himself. As he glanced out the window toward Egg Island, a dark shadow appeared in the sky.

# 16
# SERGEI'S CURIOSITY

SERGEI'S CURIOSITY was thoroughly aroused, and he asked many questions about the terrain, the vegetation, and species of birds which nested on Egg Island. He had not been there before.

"How far is Egg Island from here, Grandpa?" he queried.

"About thirty miles north of St. Michael, out in Norton Sound," Yukuniagag replied.

"Is the island as high as St. Michael, and does it have cliffs or a cave where we might anchor or tie our boat?"

"Yes, Sergei, the south end has a low cliff where the murres, puffins and seagulls nest. There's a nice beach with much driftwood on the north side. The lake on the island doesn't have an outlet, so it contains fresh water. It is very deep in the middle and around the lake there's a valley-like lowland where game birds nest their young. We can pitch our tent near there, or on the lake beach. Many kinds of wild berries grow there. Chikuk will be able to pick plenty and you and I can help her."

Chikuk listened attentively to this conversation between her husband and grandfather. Their loud voices made her son restless, so finally she had to spank him to make him lie still. When he fell asleep she went out to the kitchen to prepare their evening snack and during the meal they discussed their plans further.

Chikuk asked them to pitch the tent on the lake shore. Her husband promised her they would be on the island for a full two weeks, and furthermore, if she wished to invite one of her relatives, she could do so.

"Do you think my aunt Iglukuk would accept my invitation?" Chikuk asked grandfather. "She can make Eskimo ice cream for us."

"I'm sure she would be glad to join the berry pickers and egg gatherers. You can ask her tomorrow, Chikuk," Yukuniagag told his only granddaughter, and her husband nodded his head approvingly. Chikuk was happy.

"Sergei, will you hire another man to take my place at the restaurant next month?" Yukuniagag asked before they parted.

"This spring, beginning the latter part of February, Eskimos hunt for ugruk and ringed seals. I would like to repair my hunting outfit, mend my kayak skin covering, fix the old kayak sled, and sharpen my spearhead. I need to soak the seal-poke buoy in the water, inflate and examine it to see if there are any punctures.

Chikuk, you'll have to sew any tears in it."

"I'll be glad to sew them for you, Grandpa," answered Chikuk.

"Good. Then, when my gear is ready, my partner and I will search for ugruk out on the edge of the old ice. Maybe we'll use Egg Island as our base camp. Chikuk can bake bread and beans for me. We have to have seal oil and fresh meat. I will come home whenever I catch an ugruk, so my grandchild can enjoy the fresh meat, that is, if I'm lucky enough to catch one.'

Chikuk smiled and said, "Grandpa, if you do, I will hang the meat out to dry and take care of the blubber, and before you leave I will pack your food box. I won't forget to include your favorite tobacco and gum," she giggled.

It hadn't occurred to Sergei that he would need to give Yukuniagag a leave of absence, but he quickly realized that you can't keep an Eskimo employed when hunting season opens. It was too much a part of their very survival.

"Yes, Grandpa, you may take your leave, but only for the month of March. After that, you will have to clean out those warehouses for the supplies that will be coming in. We'll need lots of space."

"Yes, sir, boss," answered Yukuniagag with a big grin on his face.

# 17

# SUNSET FOR CHIKUK

Iglukuk was just as tired at the end of the week, or even more so, than her niece after every usable part of the *ugruk* meat, blubber, skin and intestines were cured. A day before they left for the trip to Egg Island, Iglukuk went over to Ivanoff's to help Chikuk select the parts of the fresh meat that they would take with them. She did not wish her niece to lift heavy things.

"Chik, which parts of the *ugruk* meat would you prefer to take?" Iglukuk asked as she entered the home. "Sergei can pack the groceries for us. You have to watch Stevie anyway, he's so active. Let me do some of the packing now."

"*Quyahnaa*. We'll take some dried *ugruk* meat too, fresh blubber and some of the rendered oil. You can put them in the same container. And Auntie, don't forget to bring salmonberries, *muktuk* and dried fish. I hope Sergei and Grandpa will catch a beluga at Egg Island, so we can store it away for the winter."

"Do you mean that you and I will have to preserve a whole whale while we are on the island?" Iglukuk asked her teasingly.

"Why yes, Auntie, I'm hungry for fresh boiled muktuk and *giaq* [whale intestine]. It will be nice to have a big bonfire on the beach, *ka*, Auntie? We'll have a picnic every day. The men will gather wood and fresh water for us, and we'll prepare the slabs of *muktuk* for cooking. Then I will have to keep testing the *muktuk* while it is cooking, so it will not be overly done. The men will have to build a temporary cache for storage, too."

Chikuk's musing about preserving a whale reminded Iglukuk of how much work it really was. Would the men catch one? I hope so, she thought. Then I'll have to manage everything for my dear little niece whose husband doesn't even like to eat Native food yet.

Iglukuk thought of her sister who had passed away several years earlier. If she were still alive she would be available to help Chikuk whenever it was necessary to butcher large sea animals. Delicate women were not permitted to do work of this nature. Iglukuk was glad, therefore, that she could help Chikuk in her sister's place and show her how almost the whole animal could be used for food.

"Chikuk, be sure to take all our *ulus*, large pots and the galvanized tub which will be an ideal pot to cook the *muktuk* in," Iglukuk called. "Well, here we are preparing to butcher the poor whale when it isn't even caught yet."

They both laughed as Yukuniagag and Sergei came in. They sat at the table. Sergei said, "Hot coffee would be good now, Chikuk."

"It is ready for you. My aunt and I will have the Labrador tea." They were all so excited that Chikuk and her relatives talked in their own language while Sergei listened patiently. Whenever Chikuk asked him a question, he would speak in English with a Russian accent.

Now he spoke to them all. "Tomorrow we'll get up about six o'clock. And tonight we'll bring our personal things, but not the food, down to the boat. I'll cover the load with the tent. Chikuk, will you tell your grandfolks what I've just said?"

"They understood your plan. Auntie has already packed all the food. Don't forget to pick it up in the morning; it's in the cache. Did you buy enough milk for Stevie?"

"I bought enough Cossack's food for us, Chikuk. There's one thing more you and Auntie should do: bake the bread. You can mix the ingredients and your aunt can knead the dough, then you can bake it tonight. Also, don't forget to cook beans, and later I'll add the seasonings and the meat."

"Yuku, shall we go down to the beach and wash the hull of the boat?" Iglukuk asked.

Along the way Yukuniagag invited Ahlugga to help them. This made young Stevie cry, for he, too, wanted to go down to the boat. Chikuk packed him piggyback and, gently patting her son, followed the men slowly toward the shore. He fell asleep before she reached the beach.

Chikuk went back to her home on the boardwalk, unaware that she had left her last set of footprints on the beach. She laid down her son, then herself on their bed. She was glad that her aunt was kneading the dough.

"Chikuk, be sure to take your family's water boots and raincoats to the boat in the morning. We can wear them on the boat so we'll not get soaked by the sprays," Iglukuk suggested.

"Thank you for reminding me. I'll pack them now. Will you please put the pot of beans on the stove for me? We'll have our lunch soon. You and I can have dried *ugruk* meat, and the men can have canned hash, bread and tea."

After Chikuk packed the raincoats, she reported with delight, "The weather seems to be calm, Auntie. Maybe we'll be lucky and not have a storm delay us. We'll see by morning."

Chikuk arranged the table for the men, then she said to her aunt, "Let's eat on the floor, like we used to when I was little. Food tastes better for me when I sit on the floor to eat."

After the men ate their lunch they readied their hunting and survival equipment, such as their rifles and ammunition for killing animals, and a twelve-gauge shotgun and shells for ducks.

Iglukuk and Ahlugga Kameroff went home early in the afternoon, while Sergei and Yukuniagag cleaned their guns, and sharpened their knives and the *ulus*. The fragrant smell of the bread baking permeated the house and aroused their appetite, so they had tea and bread before bedtime. While the bread was baking, Chikuk visited her neighbors and the Russian Orthodox priest. Late that night she told her husband that she had asked the priest to pray for her family. Sergei could not help but shed tears after Chikuk fell asleep. He loved his frail wife and their baby boy dearly, and had been very worried about Chikuk's lingering cough and loss of weight. He prayed, "Oh God, look upon my wife this night and give her strength, even for a little while. In Jesus' name, Amen." He felt relieved of his worry and fell asleep.

Sergei got up early and cooked the breakfast for his family while Chikuk was dressing Stevie. Chikuk appeared cheerful and more energetic.

"How's the weather, Sergei?" she asked. "Grandpa, will it be calm?"

"It is calm, with no wind out in Norton Sound. We'll have a nice trip today. Sergei, I will steer the boat while you watch the boy and Chikuk. I'm sure Stevie will be lively today. Oh, and be sure to bring an empty can! He'll need it." Yukuniagag would be their captain.

"We must be sure to bring matches, Chikuk."

"Yes, grandpa, I took a couple of cartons of them."

"All aboard everyone," Sergei the sailor announced loud and clear.

"We're ready sir." Chikuk acknowledged her husband's order by kissing him on the cheek. He, in turn, kissed his boy, who at this time was wiggling on his mother's back.

"You're a wonderful papa," Chikuk said, then led the way out the door and picked up the axe they had all forgotten to take.

She chattered continuously to her auntie and planned what she would do as soon as she got off the boat.

"I bet I'll be the first one to find duck eggs. Then we can eat fresh eggs for supper."

As they were traveling, Yukuniagag sang familiar Eskimo songs, using the "pomp-pomp" sound of the engine exhaust as a musical accompaniment. Chikuk and her aunt were amused, and laughed occasionally at the lyrical themes of his Eskimo compositions.

After three hours of traveling, Egg Island loomed before them. As they were having their lunch, Stevie fell asleep and had a long nap but upon waking he became lively again so Chikuk had to strap him in once more. He watched the birds flying overhead as they approached the island.

"Oh!" Chikuk exclaimed. "Look at all the murres, gulls, puffins, and cormorants on the cliff. I guess they're building their nests. Perhaps some already have laid their eggs. Those flying around seem to be saying, 'Stay away, stay away!'"

The men steered the boat to a landing near the cliff on the south side of the island, not far from a waterfall. The bursting wavelets on the seashore seemed to welcome them with a babbling sound. Little Stevie at once ran along the beach, but Sergei hoisted him out of the wet sand and brought him to his mother, who was gathering driftwood while Iglukuk built a fire.

The men carried the camping outfit ashore and in a short time they had pitched the tent on the higher embankment of the nearby lake. By now, all of the party had become enchanted by the beautiful landscape. Chikuk began to feel uneasy, so she walked away to hunt for duck eggs. In a short time she saw a mother eider duck sitting on its eggs. She talked to it kindly. "I won't take all your eggs, Mrs. Eider. Please fly away." The duck had eight eggs, so Chikuk took half of them. Then she took about a quarter of the eggs found in the other nearby nests—enough for her family's supper. The greedy jaeger and gulls dove at her hand as she walked back to the tent. On the way, she met Iglukuk. Her aunt had been gathering murre's eggs, which nature had painted in artistic hues of blue with black and yellow dots.

Chikuk said, "Auntie, we'll boil our eggs in a large pot. Let's have some tea now." When she and her aunt returned to the camp, Sergei set the table on a piece of oilcloth which was laid on the clean, flat rocks. They sat around it to eat their supper.

"My! These fresh eggs are real good, Chik," said Yukuniagag. "I'll have to dig a pit in the ground and line it with moss for the rest of the eggs. That way we can keep them from spoiling for several days, anyway."

When they finished eating, they romped around for a while. Then the camp stove, wood, and the grass mattresses were installed in their respective places in the tent. That first night on the island they all slept soundly and none of them were awakened by the bird calls. The people snored until Stevie woke them up by calling to his mama for his bottle. But before she fed him she went outside to rekindle the fire. Listening to and enjoying the birds' conversations which echoed from all around, she forgot about the boy and began cooking breakfast. She was happiest when she could hear this beautiful music of the birds and the sea. Suddenly she gasped and remembered Stevie. She walked over to the tent opening and peeked in.

"Oh, good, he's fallen asleep again," she said aloud. She scanned the blue-carpeted surface of the sea, and stretched her arms upward as far as she could as she gazed in awe at the bright yellow and amber rays of the sun. In the north she saw drifting icebergs being washed over by a soft, cotton-like fog. Then as she looked more closely she saw a mother seal and her furry suckling baby having its bottle. The scene reminded her of her work.

She walked over to the waterfall and filled the coffee pot, brought it back and hung it over the fire. As she did so she inhaled some wood smoke which caused her to cough. Her husband came out of the tent, sleepy-eyed, and held her.

"Are you all right? Mmm…how good the coffee smells."

"Yes. We'll soon have some sourdoughs, boiled eggs, and bacon, Sergei. Don't awaken Stevie. Let him sleep a little longer."

One by one the other members of the family came out, each one apologizing for not cooking the breakfast first. Stevie came out and sat on his great-grandpa's lap. He, too, began to chatter and point to the birds. While they were eating, Yukuniagag suddenly hushed them, pointed towards the sea and whispered, "*Siichuat*, [whales]! Come on, brother. Let's chase the belugas in my kayak," he suggested to Ahlugga, who nodded.

"The rest of you, keep quiet. Smother the fire carefully, and don't talk. Chikuk and Iglukuk, take Stevie to the tundra very quietly. Try not to step on sticks. If you do, the whales will be alarmed and will head toward the deep sea."

They parted and the women and Sergei took Stevie to the high ridge to watch the hunters. The two older men were sitting in a back-to-back position ready to fling their double-bladed paddles into action. When the whales passed the camping site, the chase began. As the men and the whales reached the shallow water on the north side of the island, Ahlugga harpooned the largest beluga. Now they tore through the water as the submerged animal pulled their kayak. Yukuniagag slid into the back of the kayak to put more weight there because the front of the craft was too heavy and caused the bow to be pulled under. Ahlugga kept the kayak from capsizing by holding his long paddle crosswise over the cockpit. At the same time, he wound the babiche onto a wooden shuttle whenever it slackened. The inflated seal poke also had slackened and surfaced above the water. This meant that the whale would soon come up for more air and spew a bloody spray of water. When it did, Ahlugga took up his spear and plunged it into the whale's side. Then, to escape being crushed by the huge beast, he had to paddle his kayak backwards as fast as his strength permitted. The whale swam round and round at a safe distance and helplessly tossed about. Yukuniagag emerged through the kayak's cockpit, took his cap off and signaled to Sergei to come over with his boat. While he was coming, Ahlugga asked Yukuniagag to shoot the whale with his rifle to make sure that it was dead before they approached closely. The three of them then went up to the floating mammal and tied its head and flukes to the side of the boat, and towed it back to the camp.

In the meantime, Chikuk and Iglukuk returned to the camp and began to gather driftwood. They laid the sticks of wood side by side on the beach parallel to and below the high tide line. By the time the men arrived, a platform was ready for them to roll the whale onto. Iglukuk met them with a bucket of fresh water. The Natives knew what this was for, but not Sergei. Chikuk explained quickly to him, then he quietly watched a rite.

After the whale was laid on the platform, Iglukuk poured the water into the whale's mouth. She gave the mammal its last drink of water to fulfill an ancient Eskimo custom, the belief that all sea mammals need to quench their thirst so that their spirit may depart.

A second phase of this traditional rite is followed to restore the hunter's energy expended during the strenuous ordeal of chasing and killing the whale. Yukuniagag and Ahlugga cut the whale's throat and held a receptacle beneath the cut to collect the blood, which each man then drank. The hunters believed that whale's blood is like the blood of a human, because whales nurse their young and have love for their families.

Conversely, despite their belief in this resemblance of whales to humans, the Eskimos did not allow their people to eat whale oil. The primitive Eskimo believed the oil to be too strong and that if consumed it might cause a hemorrhage.

Apart from what Eskimos believed about the whale, their respect for the great beast, and related customs, they derive a number of genuine benefits from the mammal, quite apart from food. For example, the whale oil is used as a detergent, especially to emulsify the rancid coagulation of oil on the seal skins when they are used as pokes. The pokes are soaked in the rendered whale oil first, then the article is washed in it. Whale blubber is therefore stored as a future supply of oil.

Yukuniagag and his uncle remembered not to waste the blubber as they butchered the whale. The rest of the group were given duties too. Sergei and Iglukuk would assist in distributing the particular cuts on wooden platforms. Sergei, with Chikuk's help, would also do the chores for all of them. Chikuk was concerned about preparing lunch for the workmen. "Auntie," she asked, "shall I cook *muktuk qiaq*?"

"That sounds good, Chik. Be sure to test the *muktuk* with the wooden tester by pushing the stick through it while it is boiling; then just plunge the *qiaq* in the boiling water, and let it boil only for a few minutes."

Chikuk was still learning how to cook fresh meat in the usual Eskimo fashion. And while Stevie was watching the butchering, she built a fire so the water would be hot enough by the time she was ready to cook the meat. When the lunch was ready she called the workers, and as they sat down, she apologized to her husband.

"I'm sorry, Sergei, I didn't prepare your lunch." She smiled. "I was so fascinated by cooking the whale meat that I guess I forgot you and Stevie."

"That's all right, Chik. I should try harder to become accustomed to the taste of whale meat and the *muktuk*, or what you call it." Chikuk then served her husband some piping hot *muktuk*, and handed him tomato catsup, salt and pepper. For the Natives, the lunch was an exceptionally delicious meal, topped with Labrador [herb] tea.

After lunch the men resumed their work and Chikuk took a short nap with Stevie. When she awoke, she joined her aunt and watched as she prepared the *muktuk* by cutting it into square blocks, without severing one from the other so the entire mass looked like a chain. Iglukuk allowed Chikuk to do some of the cutting while she was hanging the eight-foot chains. It took them the whole afternoon to prepare it all.

"Now," Iglukuk explained, "we'll have to gather some driftwood, because it takes a continuous fire to boil the muktuk. Perhaps you and I can collect some more tonight. Maybe you're too tired now."

There were still many tasks to be done. Iglukuk emptied the whale stomach, turned it inside out, washed it in saltwater and let it dry before she turned the inside back in. She then inflated the large stomach to its natural size. Chikuk watched her aunt flay the muscle covering the stomach with her special *ulu* which was not too sharp. This work was usually very tedious, but interesting to Chikuk.

"Next time your uncle or Sergei catches a whale you will be able to flay the stomach all by yourself," her aunt said smilingly.

"I'll try, Auntie, but you must watch me."

Within an hour, Iglukuk finished her work. Sergei had made additional racks and a teepee cold storage structure. By late evening all of them were tired, so they went to bed early, each one feeling thankful for the capture of the whale.

"What will we do tomorrow?" Chikuk asked.

Her aunt replied, "Pick eggs and dig for masu, then have a picnic.

"Yes…it will be a most welcome outing for all of us, eh, Sergei?"

He nodded his head. "We'll plan it tomorrow morning," he said.

In the early morning, Stevie woke them up by yelling for milk.

Sergei said, "I'll cook breakfast and prepare the milk for our boy." The boy moved over to his mother's side, and she told him the story "A Mother Mouse Hawk," which describes how a mother bird saved her children from a flood. By this time her breakfast was brought to her and the bottle for Stevie. The others had their breakfast outdoors by the campfire. She heard her aunt report to the men that the *muktuk* and inflated stomach were not quite ready for cooking.

"I'll cook the *muktuk* this evening," Iglukuk said.

That evening, as they walked back to their camp, they were carrying duck eggs, masu, sweet edible root, and winter cranberries. Chikuk's face was abnormally flushed and Sergei knew she was running a temperature when they arrived at the tent.

"Chik, here's a glass of milk. Drink it while you're resting. We'll eat later. Maybe after supper you can help your aunt cook the *muktuk*."

"Thank you." Chikuk kissed him on his cheek. This rare kiss brought tears after he went out of the tent.

At supper when they sat down, Sergei prayed aloud in his own language; his family joined him as he crossed himself and said, "Amen."

"*Annonung* [auntie], will you make *atchagluk* for us tonight?" asked Chikuk. "It would taste real good. My grandma used to let me pick cranberries and blackberries at Pastolik. Then she would make ice cream for us in the evening."

Iglukuk fulfilled her wish that evening.

Later, Chikuk spoke to her aunt. "Please wash my face with cool water and comb my hair, like my grandmother used to do; braid it too."

After her hair was combed, she fell asleep. Sergei couldn't sleep. During the night, Chikuk began to hemorrhage and more and more blood appeared in her sputum. Sergei felt fortunate to have his in-laws with him at this time of crisis. He could not have borne his suffering alone. They were more than thirty-five miles from St. Michael with no doctor on hand to help Chikuk. Soon dawn drove the darkness from the tent. The old folks prayed. Sergei took Chikuk's hands in his and pulled her up to his chest. Holding her so, he told her how their son had just caught a fish.

"I wish I had been there to watch him," she laughed. "Did he handle the fish well, Sergei?"

"Yes, but the fish kept fluttering, and he would yell, but finally he learned to hold it tight."

"When he catches another fish, have him give it to my aunt, and she'll invite some of the older people for a feast. It is our custom. The older guests will make him a prophecy and also ask

Selam Inua to bless him. Sergei, also teach him to love God; take him to our church services. I hope he'll serve God when he becomes an adult. Remember the day he was baptized?"

They both laughed and at this moment Stevie came in with the fish he had caught. He brought it over to them and said, "Mama, I caught this fish and I dragged it on the sand. My grandpa, Yuku, helped me." Since he talked in Eskimo language, Chikuk translated what he said for her husband.

"Come and hug mama, Stevie," she then said.

He crawled over the blankets and hugged his mama, and she kissed him on the nose.

"Mama, I want some milk."

"Daddy will get it for you. Sergei, will you take his fishy pants off and change his clothes?"

Iglukuk offered to do the chore for Sergei.

Chikuk made the boy crawl into bed with her for a short time. She brushed her son's hair with her hands and wondered if she would ever be with him again.

That evening, Chikuk asked her relatives to have supper in the tent, and she enjoyed their company. All she had to eat was a small helping of Eskimo ice cream and cold tea. She had no appetite. She kept holding her husband's hands, and he put cold packs on her chest.

Sergei and her relatives were with her at her death. It was not a sorrowful death, for she smiled as she took her last breath. Nevertheless, they were overwhelmed with grief, and they all wept silently for much of the rest of the morning.

When Stevie woke from a nap, he called to his mother as usual for milk, but received no response. Iglukuk picked him up and carried him outdoors, and they walked to the beach. When she came back she laid the boy on Chikuk's bed to suck his bottle—a last link to his mother.

The members of the family sat quietly outdoors, paying their respects to their loved one, then Chikuk's garments were changed for burial. The men laid her in a new cache where it was cool.

Sergei outlined his plans for his family.

"Yuku, you and I will get a coffin and a priest, Chikuk will be buried here on this beautiful island, a place she loves. We'll try to get back late this evening. Iglukuk, you take care of Stevie and pack our things. We'll all leave for home after the burial."

Late that same day, Sergei and Yuku returned with the priest. While they were having supper, Sergei suggested that they dig the grave and that his wife be buried in the morning. When they had dug the grave, Chikuk was laid in the coffin. Iglukuk said, "I will gather her favorite flowers early tomorrow." The priest offered to help her. At that moment, Sergei broke down. He kneeled, and laid his head on Chikuk's coffin pouring out his love for her. The priest tried to comfort him.

"Jesus promised in St. John, 14th chapter, that He would come to resurrect the dead and that all believing Christians would meet their Saviour and their relatives again." This reminder of his faith helped relieve the grieving man.

After the burial the next day, they returned to St. Michael. Before they reached their destination, Sergei invited his wife's great-uncle and aunt to live with him and his young son, and ended the invitation with a touching remark.

"I cannot bear to enter our home without Chikuk, and I'm sure she would want you, Auntie, to raise her son until he is old enough to care for himself."

They accepted his invitation.

# V

# STEPHAN AND MALQUAY

# 18

# ARRIVAL OF THE REVEREND KARLSON

ACCORDING TO the records of the Swedish Evangelical Mission Covenant Church of America, the Reverend Axel E. Karlson, on his first missionary journey to Caucasia, in southern Russia near the Black Sea, had been taken captive and served three years of hardship in Siberia. During this period, in the latter half of the 19th century, he studied the Russian language and learned to speak it fluently. The Reverend Karlson did not realize then that this language would be useful later during his ministry among the Eskimo people at Unalakleet. The Swedish government eventually made arrangements with the Russian leaders to release him from his confinement. Had this provision for his release failed, Karlson might have perished in Siberia, for he suffered considerably, both physically and mentally.

Shortly after his return to Sweden, the foreign mission bureau decided to establish a new mission field headquarters in the United States. It was about this time that the Reverend Karlson began making plans to establish a church in Alaska. He went to San Francisco for a year to further his training, and when that was completed, in the spring, he left by ship for St. Michael, Alaska.

St. Michael in 1887 was a booming port of entry to the majestic Yukon River, whose channels provided the principal means of travel for the gold stampeders during this period. It was a welcome sight to the missionary. After finding lodgings, he went to the restaurant to eat his supper. It was the restaurant where my grandfather, Sergei Ivanoff, was a cook for the Alaska Commercial Company. And here the Reverend Karlson first met my great-great-grandfather, Yukuniagag, who was a waiter. They all conversed in Russian.

My mother told me that it may have been my grandfather, Sergei, who advised Axel Karlson to build his church at Unalakleet. The village was located in a beautiful and quiet valley, and the village people were typical Eskimos who had not yet succumbed to the evils of the white man.

Stephan was now a school-aged boy, and Sergei was concerned about his son's future. My grandfather presented his son to the Reverend Karlson, suggesting that if Karlson needed an interpreter, Stephan was available, for he spoke both Russian and Yup'ik Eskimo fluently, in addition to English. The offer was accepted.

Karlson also met Delialuk, the chief of Unalakleet who was visiting in St. Michael. Stephan translated for both of them.

Delialuk and his brothers Maktak, Taktuk, Paniptchuk, and Nashalook gave the Reverend Karlson permission to settle and to preach the gospel in Unalakleet. That marked the beginning of my father's formal education.

It was in the late fall of 1887 that Karlson moved, with my father and grandfather, to Unalakleet, taking all his supplies with him. As the missionary and his companions first approached the village early in the morning, he noticed that none of the igloos were visible from the sea, and all that his binoculars revealed was a Russian blockhouse and a log cabin near it. He had heard that the Russians had once lived at Unalakleet, and during their sojourn many of the Natives had died from inoculations they were given. In 1867, after Alaska was sold to the United States, the Russians left.

Karlson entered the Unalakleet River, and he and his men decided they would unload their supplies as close as possible to the bank of the creek, a tributary of the river on which the village was actually situated. Karlson suggested that they anchor the ship in the channel and wait until the tide ebbed later in the day. Then they might be able to beach the boat, and it would be then easier to unload everything.

Immediately after they anchored, a few Natives appeared on the bank. The boat crew was reluctant to go ashore, so they just sat on the deck while the cook prepared their breakfast. Sergei and his son recognized the chief of Unalakleet among the Natives, and both of them waved to him. The chief returned the greeting, then turned to speak to his companions who were squatting in the tall grass. Karlson and several men, including Sergei and Stephan, then went ashore in a skiff. The chief, Delialuk, met them on the beach and, although the rest of the Natives did not seem too friendly, he extended his hand to Sergei and Stephan and spoke to them. Karlson reminded the chief that they had met at St. Michael early in the summer. The chief then pointed toward the village and said, "This is my people's village. If you do not bring harmful schemes like the Russians did in the past, you may put up your camp wherever you find a suitable place." Delialuk again gave Karlson permission to build a church at Unalakleet. My father interpreted the chief's comments for the missionary and Sergei. The newcomers then went back to the boat to eat their breakfast, and the Natives returned to their igloos.

The unloading started after the tide had gone out. When at last the boat was cleared, Karlson gave orders to leave the bulk of the supplies on the bank for the night; they had worked hard and were tired. Only their personal effects were carried to the mission grounds that Karlson had selected on the second highest ridge, just below the Eskimo village overlooking Norton Sound.

The small party pitched their tents, and after supper they all went to take a closer look at the Eskimo village, which had the appearance of a newly built settlement. The sod igloos, half above, half below ground, had been built in a semicircle, and each igloo had a tunnel entrance eight to ten yards away from the dome-shaped roof of the main structure. In the center of the semicircle of igloos was a very large igloo, which the missionary soon learned was the *kargii*. The original village had been on the opposite bank of the river, but most of the inhabitants had died, leaving only a few survivors. They had moved across the river and built the new village of Unalakleet, where Axel Karlson established his mission.

During that first year, my father and grandfather, along with the Reverend Axel Karlson, lived in tents. Early the second fall they prepared to build a log cabin. Logs were rafted down the river to the site, and some were whipsawed into planks. A number of villagers were enlisted to help with the construction, and were quite willing to work whenever they were not fishing or hunting. The Eskimos had to be taught how to use woodworking tools, but they were dexterous with their hands and learned quickly.

The walls went up rapidly and the planks were fitted to the logs to serve as joists and rafters. Sergei Ivanoff was particularly helpful in showing the builders the best way to insulate the cabin. They used dry moss to fill the joints and gaps between the logs as they laid them one on top of the other. Roof boards were placed in parallel formation on top of the rafters. On top of these boards was placed an insulating layer of thick, dry hay, and that was topped with a thick covering of peat which had been lifted from the ground in blocks. The peat was finally pressed down with a weight.

Karlson's first experience with living in this primitive environment may have been very trying for him, especially during the long, dark winters. The new cabin made life a bit easier. According to the mission records and his daily diary, he relied largely on his prayers for safety. At the point of being killed by Isaac's Point Natives, he was saved by the last chief of the Unalakleet people.

The threatening attitude of some Natives was later said to have been a result of their fear of losing their freedom. Karlson may have appeared to them as the vanguard of a new authority replacing the old Russian regime. It may also have stemmed from their misunderstanding of his God, a new God they had not seen.

In the years that followed, Karlson, through the help of Stephan, became accepted in the community and his influence grew strong. He was instrumental in the establishment of a school in Unalakleet in 1889 and was its first teacher. Here Stephan began his formal education.

The Reverend Karlson also founded an orphanage, the Covenant Mission Home, where Stephan and Malquay were brought together. The Swedish missionary thus helped shape the destiny of this Indian-Eskimo-Russian-American family.

# 19
# STEPHAN AND MALQUAY

IN TIME Sergei remarried. He and his second wife had two children, Mischa and Kiatcha. In 1902 Sergei died and Axel Karlson persuaded Mrs. Ivanoff to place her two children in his orphanage for their upbringing. There Stephan, the missionary's aide, translator, and handyman, assumed some of the parental responsibility for his half-brother and half-sister. Mischa and Kiatcha were later adopted and moved to San Francisco, where they lived throughout the period of their schooling.

Malquay, daughter of Qunigrak, was eight when her grandmother, Masu, died. She was brought to the Covenant Mission Home to be raised and educated, and there she met Stephan. Although she was taught Western values and lived in a white man's environment, she stubbornly clung to her own Eskimo culture and traditions, and continued to absorb the customs of the Unalakleet Natives. Malquay remained in the orphanage until her maturity, when she married Stephan Ivanoff.

Stephan, thoroughly imbued with the Western way of life, became a skilled carpenter, boat-builder and businessman. But he had an even stronger drive to become a missionary himself and follow in the footsteps of his mentor, Axel Karlson. He fulfilled that ambition when he entered North Park College in Illinois and earned his certificate as a minister.

After his marriage, he and Malquay built a roadhouse in Unalakleet that was well-patronized by the mail carriers who traveled the North in winter by dog sled. Stephan was an expert driver himself. One winter, word came that a whaling ship had been crushed in the ice near Barrow and the crew was in desperate need of medical aid. There was no doctor nearby. So Stephan set off with Dr. Julius Quist by dog sled from Unalakleet and made the long and difficult journey to Barrow to help the stricken seamen. The journey took two months, and during this time the capable Malquay managed the roadhouse and her husband's other business interests.

Some time later, Stephan went on a different kind of journey with Dr. Quist and another companion, Uyagak Rock, a lay preacher and relative of Malquay whom Stephan had met at the orphanage. The trio toured the United States lecturing on the educational and religious needs of the Natives of the Bering Sea coast. Before the trip Stephan had made a violin on which he performed for the audiences. Everywhere they went they collected much-needed funds for their work.

The Ivanoff family was dealt a severe blow when the chief and council of Unalakleet ordered Stephan and Malquay to leave the village. The chief said they had broken the community taboo that "no member of our village will rise in wealth over and beyond the others." Stephan, who was considered by the Eskimos as more a white man than a Native, accepted these charges. But Malquay, who had continued to cling to her Eskimo heritage, did not and was deeply jarred.

The family sold their business to a white man and, in 1907, moved north along the shore of Norton Sound to Shaktoolik, where they settled and built a log cabin. The Eskimos of this region were a scattered group, living separately with no organized village. Stephan and Malquay soon built a new roadhouse. He then convinced the Eskimos to establish a real village, to give up their old sod houses and live in new log cabins which he would help them build. And they would apply to the Covenant Church to establish a church in the new village of Shaktoolik.

A school was part of Stephan's plan for the village, too. His half-brother Mischa, educated as a teacher, had returned to Unalakleet from San Francisco and had married Alice Umigichork. Stephan successfully applied to the U.S. Bureau of Education to hire Mischa to start a school at Shaktoolik. In the spring of 1909 the school opened in a tent, and it was here that Stephan's only daughter, Emily (Ticasuk), began her education. Kiatcha had also returned to Unalakleet where she taught music and served as an interpreter for the other teachers in the school.

As a minister of the Covenant Church, Stephan Ivanoff served for twenty-eight years as president of the Native conferences. The conferences were held at intervals in the villages surrounding Norton Sound and beyond. These evangelical gatherings were not only a time for fellowship and spiritual reunion, but carried out the business of appointing lay ministers, formed plans for the rotation of those who needed a transfer, and raised funds to pay the ministers' salaries. He also served a term as United States Commissioner for the district.

Stephan and Malquay lived together for sixty-five years. In all that time Malquay continued to follow, as far as was possible, the customs of her Eskimo heritage, for she recognized their value. Her husband, on the other hand, held to the white man's ways in which he was brought up. Malquay, with patience and understanding, disciplined his restless and ambitious traits. They were happy together throughout their years.

Four children were born to this couple, three sons and a daughter. The first son, Alvin, died in Shaktoolik in 1931. Henry, their second son, was lost at sea off Shishmaref in 1934. The third son, Paul, died a year after his father.

After a long and prosperous and generous life, Stephan Ivanoff died in 1967 at the age of eighty-two.

I am Ticasuk, their daughter, the last child of Stephan and Malquay of the lineage of Alluyagnak of Unalakleet. I have three children...

# APPENDIX I
# SIX GENERATIONS OF TICASUK'S EXTENDED FAMILY

Sergei Ivanoff, a Russian citizen who came to Alaska with his brother about 1860, married Chikuk, a Yup'ik Eskimo and daughter of Chalavaluk. Chalavaluk, daughter of Mr. and Mrs. Yukuniagag, gave up her daughter rather than kill her, and is regarded as the person who stopped the practice of infanticide among the Yup'ik on the lower Yukon River.

Sergei and Chikuk had one child, a son named Stephan, born about 1885. Chikuk died when Stephan was a very small boy and her great-aunt Iglukuk (sister of Mrs. Yukuniagag) and great-uncle Ahlugga Kameroff helped Sergei raise Stephan.

Several years after Chikuk's death, Sergei married his housekeeper, by whom he had a son, Mischa, born about 1887, and a daughter, Kiatcha, born about 1889. After Kiatcha's birth, the family moved from St. Michael to Unalakleet, where Sergei died in 1902.

Sergei's and Chikuk's son Stephan married Malquay in Unalakleet. Malquay was the daughter of Qunigrak, whose cousin was chief of the village. Her paternal grandmother was Masu and her sister Amak.

Stephan and Malquay Ivanoff had four children: Paul, Henry, Alvin, and Emily (Ticasuk). Each has children living today.

# APPENDIX II: TICASUK'S FAMILY TREE

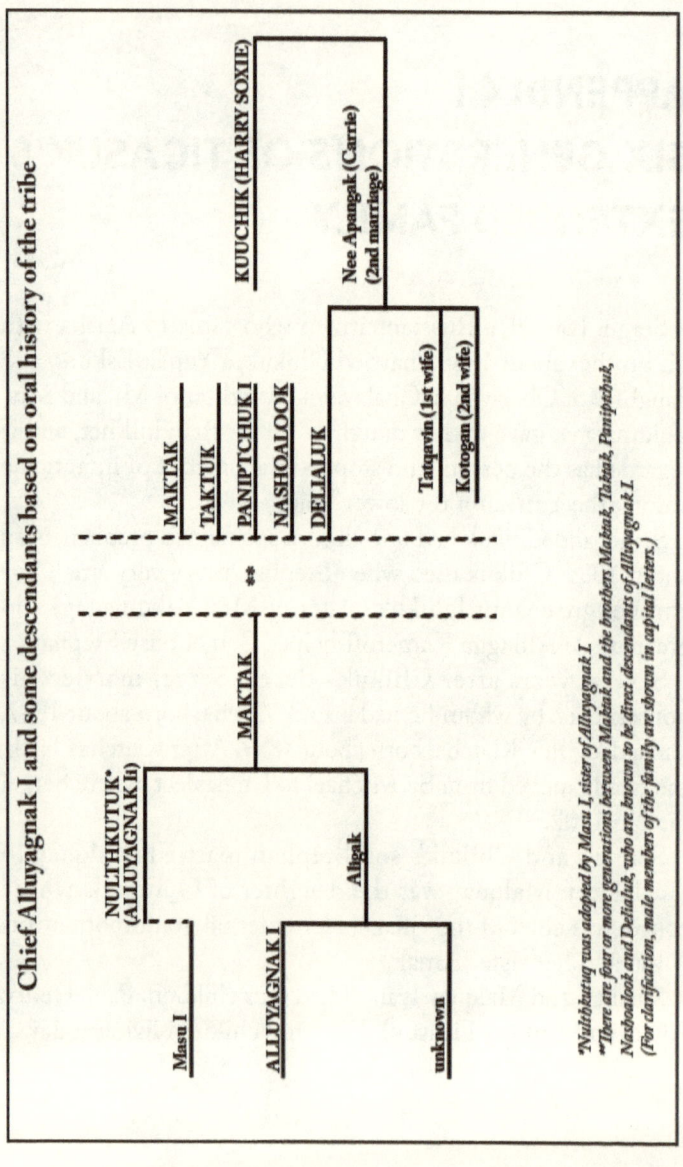

Chief Alluyagnak I and some descendants based on oral history of the tribe

Masu I

ALLUYAGNAK I

unknown

NULTHKUTUK*
(ALLUYAGNAK Ii)

Aligak

MAKTAK

**

MAKTAK
TAKTUK
PANIPTCHUK I
NASHOALOOK
DELLALUK

Tatqavin (1st wife)
Kotogan (2nd wife)

KUUCHIK (HARRY SOXIE)

Nee Apangak (Carrie)
(2nd marriage)

*Nulthkutuq was adopted by Masu I, sister of Alluyagnak I.
**There are four or more generations between Maktak and the brothers Maktak, Taktuk, Paniptchuk, Nashoalook and Dellaluk, who are known to be direct descendants of Alluyagnak I.
(For clarification, male members of the family are shown in capital letters.)

# APPENDIX II (CONTINUED)

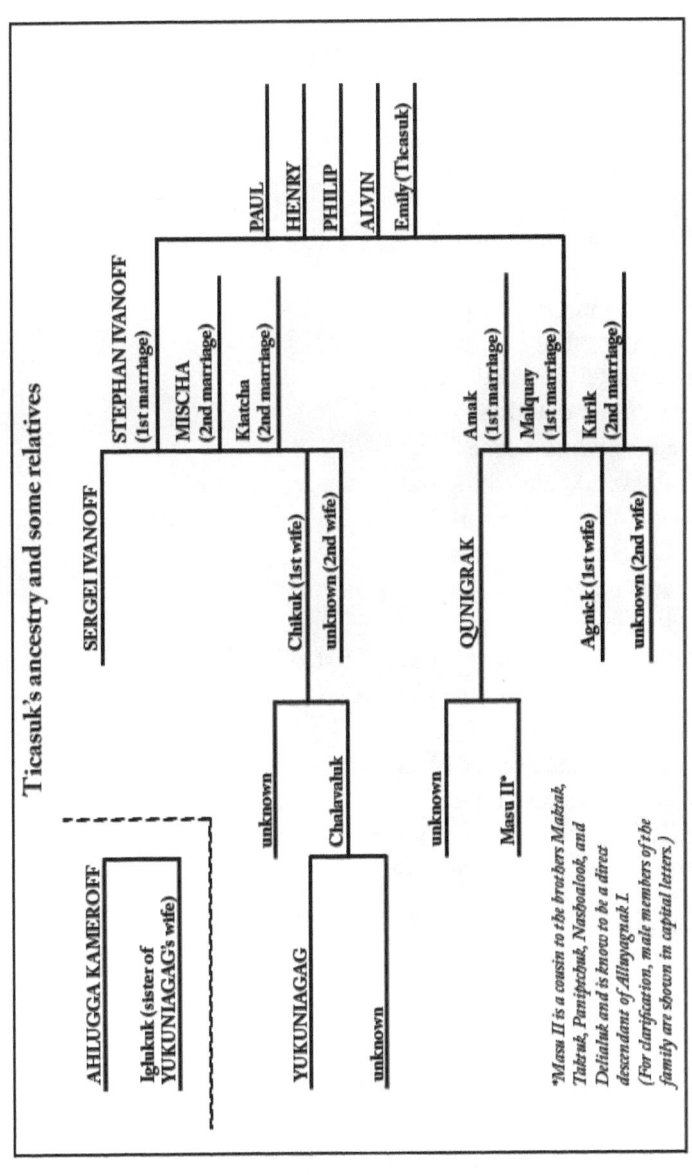

Ticasuk's ancestry and some relatives

SERGEI IVANOFF

STEPHAN IVANOFF (1st marriage)

MISCHA (2nd marriage)

Kiatcha (2nd marriage)

PAUL
HENRY
PHILIP
ALVIN
Emily (Ticasuk)

Chikuk (1st wife)

unknown (2nd wife)

unknown

Chalavaluk

AHLUGGA KAMEROFF

Iglukuk (sister of YUKUNIAGAG's wife)

YUKUNIAGAG

unknown

QUNIGRAK

Amak (1st marriage)

Malquay (1st marriage)

Kitrik (2nd marriage)

Agnick (1st wife)

unknown (2nd wife)

unknown

Masu II*

*Masu II is a cousin to the brothers Mabruk, Tabruk, Pamiptchuk, Nasboalook, and Defialuk and is know to be a direct descendant of Alltavagnak I

(For clarification, male members of the family are shown in capital letters.)

# IÑUPIAQ-ENGLISH GLOSSARY

Aaoag: yes
Achaagluk: dessert made from fermented sweet beachgrass
  and wild strawberries
Agnak: a female
Ah: yes
Amii: all right
Annonung: aunt, auntie
Arig'a: fine
Asiakpanjit: big berries, or apples and oranges
Atausiq: one
Atchagluk: Iñupiaq ice cream
Banuning: daughter
Beluga: white whale
Caluxverak: a birthing hut
Copaniskaks: the Russian-American Company (later Alaska
  Commercial Company)
Gamaka: boots
Igloo: house
Igunak: a celebrated Iñupiaq feast, with ugruk the main food
Iksi nai chute: They won't hurt you
Kaq'qeen: come
Kargii: council house or main community house
Kayak: closed skin boat
Kilak'lugok: window in the roof of an igloo, entrance for a
  good spirit as well as a skylight and fireplace vent
Malluk: two
Muktuk: whale's outer skin, a delicacy
Naluaqmite: people of the bleached sealskin, or white men
Newborik: second wife
Pinasut: three
Qiaq: outer muscle of a whale's intestine, an Eskimo food

Quyahnaa: thanks, thank you
Selam Inua: Ruler of the Sky
Siichaut: whales
Sisamat: four
Tavra: enough
Tusiq: St. Michael
Ugruk: bearded seal
Ulu: woman's knife
Umiak: large, open skin boat

## ABOUT THE AUTHOR

TICASUK (Emily Ivanoff Brown) died May 3, 1982, in Fairbanks, Alaska, just a week before she was to have received an honorary Doctor of Humanities degree from the University of Alaska. She had already earned two Bachelor of Arts degrees and a Master's degree from that school—all after her sixtieth birthday. She spent her life striving to learn and pass on her knowledge to others.

Ticasuk was born in Unalakleet, Alaska, in 1904. Her mother was Eskimo and her father was of Russian-American-English heritage. After earning her teacher's certificate in Oregon, she taught in Kotzebue for two years and then attended nursing school in Seattle so that she could work on correcting health problems in Alaska Native villages. She married Robert Brown, whom she had met in Seattle, and they had three sons. She taught in the Kotzebue and Unalakleet schools for over thirty years and was an early promoter of bilingual education.

Emily Ivanoff Brown wrote three books after *The Roots of Ticasuk*. Her books have become favorites among a wide readership, from young students to the general adult reader as well as the anthropologist.

She received many awards for her work in education and preserving Native culture: the Governor's Award, Alaskan of the Year, 1969; Distinguished Alumnus of the Year, University of Alaska, 1970; Woman of the Year, National Federation of Press Women, 1974; and a Presidential Commendation for "exceptional service to others in the finest American tradition," from President Nixon. She received her honorary Doctor of Humanities degree posthumously, six days after her death.

Concerned about the Westernization of the Inupiat people, and sustained by her belief in the importance of preserving the traditional Eskimo way of life, Ticasuk said, "I wish that my descendants may know who their people are."

## NORTHWEST COLLECTION TITLES

*The Northwest Collection is an ongoing series of titles that represent the rich literary history of the Pacific Northwest, published in editions featuring introductions and insights from contemporary writers. All Northwest Collection titles can be purchased at www.propellerbooks.com*

**Sheila Evans** The Northport Stories
**Alan Hart** The Undaunted
**Evan P. Schneider** A Simple Machine, Like the Lever
**Mary Rechner** Nine Simple Patterns for Complicated Women
**Ticasuk** The Roots of Ticasuk

www.ingramcontent.com/pod-product-compliance
Lightning Source LLC
Chambersburg PA
CBHW031417120626
46545CB00006B/2154